THE KINGFISHER BOOK OF
FUNNY
POEMS

Research by Dr. Hilary McGough

KINGFISHER
Larousse Kingfisher Chambers Inc.
80 Maiden Lane
New York, New York 10038
www.kingfisherpub.com

First published in the U.K. as *The Kingfisher Book of Comic Verse* 1986
This edition first published in the U.S. by Kingfisher 2002
10 9 8 7 6 5 4 3 2 1

LIBRARY OF CONGRESS CATALOGING-IN-PUBLICATION DATA
has been applied for.

ISBN 0-7534-5480-7

Printed in India

1TR/1201/THOM/-(FR)120INDWF

THE KINGFISHER BOOK OF
FUNNY
POEMS

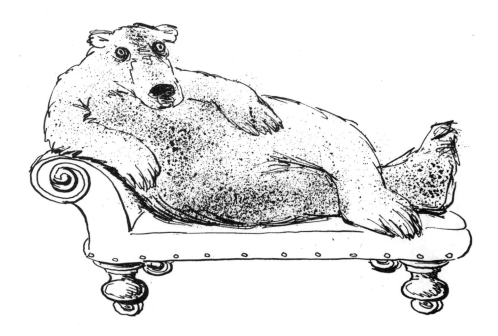

SELECTED BY ROGER McGOUGH
ILLUSTRATED BY CAROLINE HOLDEN

KINGFISHER
NEW YORK

CONTENTS

FARAWAY PLACES

FAIR WARNINGS

CHEW ON THIS

HANDS, KNEES, AND BUMPS

MEET THE FOLKS

IS ANYB-B-BODY THERE?

ALL CREATURES GREAT . . .

. . . AND SMALLISH

SQUARE PEGS

INTRODUCTION

I BELIEVE THAT ALL CHILDREN ARE POETS before **education** kicks in. By this I mean that young minds make bizarre and wonderful connections between things that appear unconnected: *When lit, candles cry. Once a month, bits fall off the moon. Old people walk slowly because they have plenty of time.* Then we adults come along, either as parents or teachers, and make sense of the world for them. But by explaining it rationally we also take away some of the magic, and the humor.

Many of the poems in this collection will hopefully make you laugh out loud, or at least giggle and smile. But not all—for senses of humor vary. One person's funny bone may be somebody else's not so funny bone. What all these poets have in common is the trick (retained from childhood) of seeing the world in an off-the-wall sort of way. Funny, peculiar, outrageous, uproarious—but always interesting.

Above all, there is a love of language here. Poems to cheer us up and to celebrate the fact that poetry can make our spirits soar.

Roger Mc Gough

London, 2002

SOME PEOPLE NEVER LEARN

THE LEADER

I wanna be the leader
I wanna be the leader
Can I be the leader?
Can I? I can?
Promise? Promise?
Yippee, I'm the leader
I'm the leader

OK what shall we do?

Roger McGough

14

LOOK OUT!

The witches mumble horrid chants,
You're scolded by five thousand aunts,
   A Martian pulls a fearsome face
   And hurls you into Outer Space,
You're tied in front of whistling trains,
A tomahawk has sliced your brains,
   The tigers snarl, the giants roar,
   You're sat on by a dinosaur.
In vain you're shouting 'Help' and 'Stop',
The walls are spinning like a top,
   The earth is melting in the sun
   And all the horror's just begun.
And, oh, the screams, the thumping hearts
That awful night before school starts.

Max Fatchen

WHATIF

Last night, while I lay thinking here,
Some Whatifs crawled inside my ear
And pranced and partied all night long
And sang their same old Whatif song:
Whatif I'm dumb in school?
Whatif they've closed the swimming pool?
Whatif I get beat up?
Whatif there's poison in my cup?
Whatif I start to cry?
Whatif I get sick and die?
Whatif I flunk that test?
Whatif green hair grows on my chest?
Whatif nobody likes me?
Whatif a bolt of lightning strikes me?
Whatif I don't grow taller?
Whatif my head starts getting smaller?
Whatif the fish won't bite?
Whatif the wind tears up my kite?
Whatif they start a war?
Whatif my parents get divorced?
Whatif the bus is late?
Whatif my teeth don't grow in straight?
Whatif I tear my pants?
Whatif I never learn to dance?
Everything seems swell, and then
The nighttime Whatifs strike again!

Shel Silverstein

DISTRACTED THE MOTHER SAID TO HER BOY

Distracted the mother said to her boy,
'Do you try to upset and perplex and annoy?
Now, give me four reasons – and don't play the fool –
Why you shouldn't get up and get ready for school.'

Her son replied slowly, 'Well, mother, you see,
I can't stand the teachers and they detest me;
And there isn't a boy or a girl in the place
That I like or, in turn, that delights in my face.'

'And I'll give you two reasons,' she said, 'why you ought
Get yourself off to school before you get caught;
Because, first, you are forty, and, next, you young fool,
It's your job to be there.
You're the head of the school.'

Gregory Harrison

SUPPLY TEACHER

Here is the rule for what to do
Whenever your teacher has the flu,
Or for some other reason takes to her bed
And a different teacher comes instead.

When this visiting teacher hangs up her hat,
Writes the date on the board, does this or that;
Always remember, you must say this:
'*Our* teacher never does that, Miss!'

When you want to change places or wander about,
Or feel like getting the guinea-pig out,
Never forget, the message is this:
'*Our* teacher always lets us, Miss!'

Then, when your teacher returns next day
And complains about the paint or clay,
Remember these words, you just say this:
'That *other* teacher told us to, Miss!'

Allan Ahlberg

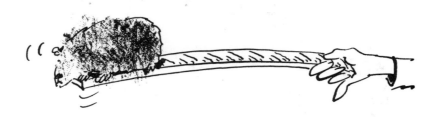

THE HERO

Slowly with bleeding nose and aching wrists
After tremendous use of feet and fists
He rises from the dusty schoolroom floor
And limps for solace to the girl next door
Boasting of kicks and punches, cheers and noise,
And far worse damage done to bigger boys.

Robert Graves

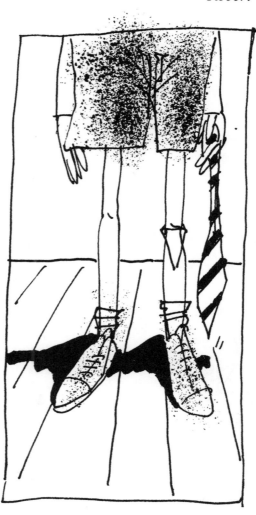

SHIRLEY SAID

Who wrote 'kick me' on my back?
Who put a spider in my mac?
Who's the one who pulls my hair?
Tries to trip me everywhere?
Who runs up to me and strikes me?
That boy there – I think he likes me.

Denis Doyle

QUESTIONS

Do trains get tired of running
And woodworms tired of holes
Do tunnels tire of darkness
And stones of being so old?

Do shadows tire of sunshine
And puddles tire of rain?
And footballs tire of kicking
Does Peter tire of Jane?

Does water tire of spilling
And fires of being too hot
And smells get tired of smelling
And chickenpox – of spots?

I do not know the answers
I'll ask them all one day . . .
But I get tired of reading
And I've done enough today.

Peter Dixon

THE ANSWERS

'When did the world begin and how?'
I asked a lamb, a goat, a cow:

'What's it all about and why?'
I asked a hog as he went by:

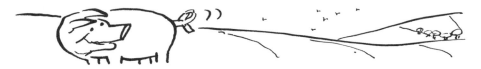

'Where will the whole thing end, and when?'
I asked a duck, a goose, a hen:

And I copied all the answers too,
A quack, a honk, an oink, a moo.

Robert Clairmont

PICKING TEAMS

When we pick teams in the playground,
Whatever the game might be,
There's always somebody left till last
And usually it's me.

I stand there looking hopeful
And tapping myself on the chest,
But the captains pick the others first,
Starting, of course, with the best.

Maybe if teams were sometimes picked
Starting with the worst,
Once in his life a boy like me
Could end up being first!

Allan Ahlberg

COME ON IN THE WATER'S LOVELY

Come on in the water's lovely
It isn't really cold at all
Of course you'll be quite safe up this end
If you hold tight to the wall.

Of course that fat boy there won't drown you
He's too busy drowning Gail.
Just imagine you're a tadpole.
I *know* you haven't got a tail.

Oh come on in the water's lovely
Warm and clear as anything
All the bottom tiles are squiggly
And your legs like wriggly string.

Come on in the water's lovely
It's no good freezing on the side
How do you know you're going to drown
Unless you've really tried.

What? You're really going to do it?
You'll jump in on the count of three?
Of course the chlorine doesn't blind you
Dive straight in and you'll soon see.

One – it isn't really deep at all.
Two – see just comes to my chin.
Three – oh there's the bell for closing time
And just as you jumped in!

Gareth Owen

TODAY IS VERY BORING

Today is very boring,
it's a very boring day,
there is nothing much to look at,
there is nothing much to say,
there's a peacock on my sneakers,
there's a penguin on my head,
there's a dormouse on my doorstep,
I am going back to bed.

Today is very boring,
it is boring through and through,
there is absolutely nothing
that I think I want to do,
I see giants riding rhinos,
and an ogre with a sword,
there's a dragon blowing smoke rings,
I am positively bored.

Today is very boring,
I can hardly help but yawn,
there's a flying saucer landing
in the middle of my lawn,
a volcano just erupted
less than half a mile away,
and I think I felt an earthquake,
it's a very boring day.

Jack Prelutsky

COLOUR OF MY DREAMS

I'm a really rotten reader
the worst in all the class,
the sort of rotten reader
that makes you want to laugh.

I'm last in all the readin' tests,
my score's not on the page
and when I read to teacher
she gets in such a rage.

She says I cannot form my words
she says I can't build up
and that I don't know phonics
-- and don't know c-a-t from k-u-p.

They say that I'm dyxlectic
(that's a word they've just found out)
. . . but when I get some plasticine
    I know what that's about.

I make these scary monsters
I draw these secret lands
and get my hair all sticky
and paint on all me hands.

I make these super models,
I build these smashing towers
that reach up to the ceiling
– and take me hours and hours.

I paint these lovely pictures
in thick green drippy paint
that gets all on the carpet –
and makes the cleaners faint.

I build great magic forests
weave bushes out of string
and paint pink panderellos
and birds that really sing.

I play my world of real believe
I play it every day
and teachers stand and watch me
but don't know what to say.

They give me diagnostic tests,
they try out reading schemes,
but none of them will ever know
the colour of my dreams.

Peter Dixon

29

A POEM

a poem moves down a page

faster than a novel

Richard Meltzer

THERE ARE NOT ENOUGH OF US

How much verse is magnificent?
Point oh oh oh one per cent.
How much poetry is second-rate?
Around point oh oh oh oh eight.
How much verse is botched hotch-potch?
Ninety-eight per cent by my watch.
How much poetry simply bores?
None of mine and all of yours.

Adrian Mitchell

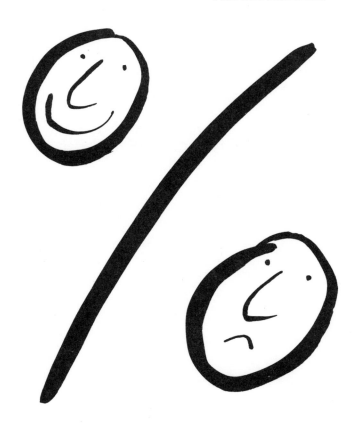

OIC

I'm in a 10der mood today
    & feel poetic, 2;
4 fun I'll just – off a line
    & send it off 2 U.

I'm sorry you've been 6 o long;
    Don't B disconsol8;
But bear your ills with 42de,
    & they won't seem so gr8.

Anonymous

ARITHMETICKLE

I'd rather go fishin'
Than do long division,
Or be stuck in traction
Than deal with subtraction.
I need a vacation
From multiplication.
In my poor condition
I can't do addition.

Let's leave mathematics
Forgotten in attics!

Douglas Florian

THE TRADITIONAL GRAMMARIAN AS POET

Haiku, you ku, he,
She, or it kus, we ku, you
Ku, they ku. Thang ku.

Ted Hipple

XMAS FOR THE BOYS

A clockwork skating Wordsworth on the ice,
An automatic sermonising Donne,
A brawling Marlowe shaking out the dice,
A male but metaphysical Thom Gunn.
Get them all now – the latest greatest set
Of all the Poets, dry to sopping wet.

A mad, ferocious, disappointed Swift
Being beaten by a servant in the dark.
Eliot going up to Heaven in a lift,
Shelley going overboard, just for a lark.
Although the tempo and the talent varies
Now is the time to order the whole series.

An electronic Milton, blind as a bat,
A blood-spitting consumptive Keats,
Tennyson calmly raising a tall hat,
Swinburne being whipped in certain dark back streets.
All working models, correct from head to toe –
But Shakespeare's extra, as you ought to know.

Gavin Ewart

STREEMIN

im in the botom streme
wich means im not britgh

dont lik readin
cant hardly write

But all these divishns
arnt reelly fair

Look at the cemtery
no streemin there

Roger McGough

ROBINSON CRUSOE

Wrecked castaway
   On lonely strand
Works hard all day
   To tame the land,
Takes times to pray;
   Makes clothes by hand.

For eighteen years
   His skill he plies,
Then lo! A footprint
   He espies –
'Thank God it's Friday!'
   Crusoe cries.

Take heart from his
   Example, chums:
Work hard, produce;
   Complete your sums;
Eventually,
   Friday comes.

Maurice Sagoff

I DID A BAD THING ONCE

I did a bad thing once.
I took this money from my mother's purse
For bubble gum.
What made it worse,
She bought me some
For being good, while I'd been vice versa
So to speak – that made it worser.

Allan Ahlberg

REPORT CARD

My school grades sent my father reeling.
He blew his top. He hit the ceiling.
We patched him up and now he's healing.

Douglas Florian

WHAT I FOUND IN MY DESK

A ripe peach with an ugly bruise,
a pair of stinky tennis shoes,
a day-old ham-and-cheese on rye,
a swimsuit that I left to dry,
a pencil that glows in the dark,
some bubble gum found in the park,
a paper bag with cookie crumbs,
an old kazoo that barely hums,
a spelling test I almost failed,
a letter that I should have mailed,
and one more thing, I must confess,
a note from teacher: Clean This Mess!!!!

Bruce Lansky

DOWN BY THE SCHOOL GATE

There goes the bell
it's half past three
and down by the school gate
you will see . . .

. . . ten mums in coats, talking
nine babes in prams, squawking
eight dads their cars parking
seven dogs on leads barking

six toddlers all squabbling
five Grans on bikes wobbling
four child-minders running
three bus drivers sunning

two teenagers dating
one lollipop man waiting . . .

The school is out,
it's half past three
and the first to the school gate
. . . is me!

Wes Magee

HOMEWORK! OH, HOMEWORK!

Homework! Oh, homework!
I hate you! You stink!
I wish I could wash you
away in the sink,
if only a bomb
would explode you to bits.
Homework! Oh, homework!
You're giving me fits.

I'd rather take baths
with a man-eating shark,
or wrestle a lion
alone in the dark,
eat spinach and liver,
pet ten porcupines,
than tackle the homework
my teacher assigns.

Homework! Oh, homework!
You're last on my list,
I simply can't see
why you even exist,
if you just disappeared
it would tickle me pink.
Homework! Oh, homework!
I hate you! You stink!

Jack Prelutsky

WHY MY HOMEWORK IS MISSING

Deep inside my wooden desk
Lurks a monster most grotesque.
It ate my pencil and my pen,
My composition book, and THEN
It started rattling
              clattering
                  hissing.
And THAT is why
My homework is missing.

Douglas Florian

NEW SIGHTS

I like to see a thing I know
Has not been seen before;
That's why I cut my apple through
To look into the core.

It's nice to think, though many an eye
Has seen the ruddy skin,
Mine is the very first to spy
The five brown pips within.

Anonymous

ON THE NING NANG NONG

On the Ning Nang Nong
Where the Cows go Bong!
And the Monkeys all say Boo!
There's a Nong Nang Ning
Where the trees go Ping!
And the tea pots Jibber Jabber Joo.
On the Nong Ning Nang
All the mice go Clang!
And you just can't catch 'em when they do!
So it's Ning Nang Nong!
Cows go Bong!
Nong Nang Ning!
Trees go Ping!
Nong Ning Nang!
The mice go Clang!
What a noisy place to belong,
Is the Ning Nang Ning Nang Nong!!

Spike Milligan

45

THE FASTEST TRAIN IN THE WORLD

Tokyo to Kyoto
  tokyotokyoto
kyotokyotokyotokyo
  tokyotokyoto

Keith Bosley

There was a young girl of Asturias
Whose temper was frantic and furious
She used to throw eggs
At her grandmother's legs –
A habit unpleasant and curious

Anonymous

There was an old person of Fratton
Who would go to church with his hat on.
'If I wake up,' he said,
'With a hat on my head,
I will know that it hasn't been sat on.'

Anonymous

OF PYGMIES, PALMS AND PIRATES

Of pygmies, palms and pirates,
Of islands and lagoons,
Of blood-bespotted frigates,
Of crags and octoroons,
Of whales and broken bottles,
Of quicksands cold and grey,
Of ullages and dottles,
I have no more to say.

Of barley, corn and furrows,
Of farms and turf that heaves
Above such ghostly burrows
As twitch on summer eves
Of fallow-land and pasture,
Of skies both pink and grey,
I made a statement last year
And have no more to say.

Mervyn Peake

O'ER SEAS THAT HAVE NO BEACHES

O'er seas that have no beaches
To end their waves upon,
I floated with twelve peaches,
A sofa and a swan.

The blunt waves crashed above us
The sharp waves burst around,
There was no one to love us,
No hope of being found –

Where, on the notched horizon
So endlessly a-drip,
I saw all of a sudden
No sign of any ship.

Mervyn Peake

THE TROUBLE WITH GERANIUMS

The trouble with geraniums
is that they're much too red!
The trouble with my toast is that
it's far too full of bread.

The trouble with a diamond
is that it's much too bright.
The same applies to fish and stars
and the electric light.

The trouble with the stars I see
lies in the way they fly.
The trouble with myself is all
self-centred in the eye.

The trouble with my looking-glass
is that it shows me, me:
there's trouble in all sorts of things
where it should never be.

Mervyn Peake

'TWAS IN THE MONTH OF LIVERPOOL

'Twas in the month of Liverpool
In the city of July,
The snow was raining heavily,
The streets were very dry.
The flowers were sweetly singing,
The birds were in full bloom,
As I went down the cellar
To sweep an upstairs room.

Anonymous

THE BLUE ROOM

My room is blue, the carpet's blue,
The chairs are blue, the door's blue too.
A blue bird flew in yesterday,
I don't know if it's flown away.

Richard Edwards

SHED IN SPACE

My Grandad Lewis
On my mother's side
Had two ambitions.
One was to take first prize
For shallots at the village show
And the second
Was to be a space commander.

Every Tuesday
After I'd got their messages,
He'd lead me with a wink
To his garden shed
And there, amongst the linseed
And the sacks of peat and horse manure
He'd light his pipe
And settle in his deck chair.
His old eyes on the blue and distant
That no one else could see,
He'd ask,
'Are we A O.K. for lift off?'
Gripping the handles of the lawn mower
I'd reply:
'A O.K.'

And then
Facing the workbench,
In front of shelves of paint and creosote
And racks of glistening chisels
He'd talk to Mission Control.
'Five-Four-Three-Two-One-Zero –
We have lift off.
This is Grandad Lewis talking,
Do you read me?
Britain's first space shed
is rising majestically into orbit
From its launch pad
In the allotments
In Lakey Lane.'

And so we'd fly,
Through timeless afternoons
Till tea time came,
Amongst the planets
And mysterious suns,
While the world
Receded like a dream:
Grandad never won
That prize for shallots,
But as the captain
Of an intergalactic shed
There was no one to touch him.

Gareth Owen

BILLY THE KID

Billy was a bad man
And carried a big gun,
He was always chasing women
And kept 'em on the run.

He shot men every morning
Just to make a morning meal –
If his gun ran out of bullets
He killed them with cold steel.

He kept folks in hot water,
And he stole from many a stage,
When his gut was full of liquor
He was always in a rage.

But one day he met a man
Who was a whole lot badder –
And now he's dead –
And we ain't none the sadder.

Anonymous

WENT TO THE RIVER

Went to the river, couldn't get across,
Paid five dollars for an old gray hoss.
Hoss wouldn't pull so I traded for a bull.
Bull wouldn't holler so I traded for a dollar.
Dollar wouldn't pass so I threw it on the grass.
Grass wouldn't grow so I traded for a hoe.
Hoe wouldn't dig so I traded for a pig.
Pig wouldn't squeal so I traded for a wheel.
Wheel wouldn't run so I traded for a gun.
Gun wouldn't shoot so I traded for a boot.
Boot wouldn't fit so I thought I'd better quit.
So I quit.

Anonymous

GOOD BEDS

Grandmother's couch
Kangaroo pouch
Soft mushy chair
Big friendly bear
A huge stack of hay
Your mom's macramé
A dozen koalas
A half-million dollars

Douglas Florian

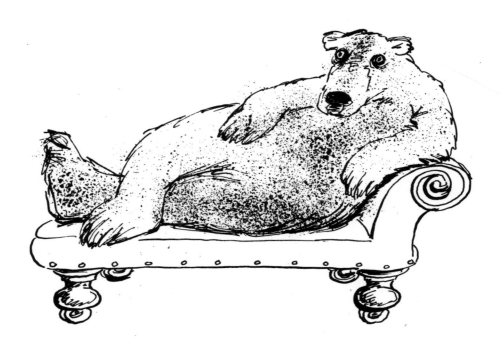

BAD BEDS

Bench in a park
Mouth of a shark
Garbage pails
Bed of nails
Elephant's trunk
In range of a skunk
Underneath birds
Near stampeding herds

Douglas Florian

I'VE TAKEN TO MY BED

I've taken to my bed
(And my bed has taken to me)
We're getting married in the spring
How happy we shall be

We'll raise lots of little bunks
A sleeping-bag or two
Take my advice: find a bed that's nice
Lie down and say: 'I love you.'

Roger McGough

AT THE HOUSEFLY PLANET

Upon the housefly planet
the fate of the human is grim:
for what he does here to the housefly,
the fly does there unto him.

To paper with honey cover
the humans there adhere,
while others are doomed to hover
near death in vapid beer.

However, one practice of humans
the flies will not undertake:
they will not bake us in muffins
nor swallow us by mistake.

Christian Morgenstern

ON SOME OTHER PLANET

On some other planet
near some other star,
there's a music-loving alien
who has a green estate car.

On some other planet
on some far distant world,
there's a bright sunny garden
where a cat lies curled.

On some other planet
a trillion miles away,
there are parks and beaches
where the young aliens play.

On some other planet
in another time zone,
there are intelligent beings
who feel very much alone.

On some other planet
one that we can't see,
there must be one person
who's a duplicate of me.

John Rice

NUTTY NURSERY RHYMES

'Jump over the moon?' the cow declared,
  'With a dish and a spoon. Not me.
I need a suit and a rocket ship
  And filmed by the BBC.

'I want a roomy capsule stall
  For when I blast away,
And an astronaut as a dairymaid
  And a bale of meadow hay.'

She gave a twitch of her lazy rump,
  'Space travel takes up time.
I certainly don't intend to jump
  For a mad old nursery rhyme.'

Max Fatchen

THE OWL AND THE ASTRONAUT

The owl and the astronaut
Sailed through space
In their intergalactic ship
They kept hunger at bay
With three pills a day
And drank through a protein drip.
The owl dreamed of mince
And slices of quince
And remarked how life had gone flat;
'It may be all right
To fly faster than light
But I preferred the boat and the cat.'

Gareth Owen

SKY IN THE PIE!

Waiter, there's a sky in my pie
Remove it at once if you please
You can keep your incredible sunsets
I ordered meatloaf and cheese

I can't stand nightingales singing
Or clouds all burnished with gold
The whispering breeze is disturbing the peas
And making my fries go all cold

I don't care if the chef is an artist
Whose paintings are thought to be great
I wanted meat and hot gravy
Not the Universe heaped on my plate

OK I'll try just a spoonful
I suppose I've got nothing to lose
Mm . . . the colours quite tickle the palette
With a blend of delicate hues

The sun has a custardy flavour
And the clouds are as light as air
And the wind a chewier texture
(With a hint of cinnamon there?)

This sky is simply delicious
Why haven't I tried it before?
I can chew my way through to Eternity
And still have room left for more

Having acquired a taste for the Cosmos
I'll polish this sunset off soon
I can't wait to tuck into the night sky
Waiter! Please bring me the Moon!

Roger McGough

O's

A little b●y called R●bert R●se,
Whenever reading verse ●r pr●se
W●uld ●ften c●l●ur in the O's.
He used a pencil f●r the j●b
And made each O an ●di●us bl●b.

Unhappily f●r R●bert R●se,
He caught a strange disease
Where O's appeared between his t●es
And then behind his knees.

His elb●w, thr●at and then his n●se
Were sl●wly ●vergr●wn with O's,
Then suddenly, ●h w●e, alack!
Th●se ●vals went c●mpletely black.

He died ●f c●urse, which ●nly sh●ws
Y●u sh●uldn't mess ar●und with O's!

Doug Macleod

KITTY

Isn't it a
Dreadful pity
What became of
Dreamy Kitty,
Noticing the
Moon above her,
Not
   the
      missing
         man-hole
          cover?

Colin West

KENNETH
who was too fond of bubble-gum and met an untimely end

The chief defect of Kenneth Plumb
Was chewing too much bubble-gum.
He chewed away with all his might,
Morning, evening, noon and night.
Even (oh, it makes you weep)
Blowing bubbles in his sleep.
He simply couldn't get enough!
His face was covered with the stuff.
As for his teeth – oh, what a sight!
It was a wonder he could bite.
His loving mother and his dad
Both remonstrated with the lad.
Ken repaid them for the trouble
By blowing yet another bubble.

Twas no joke. It isn't funny
Spending all your pocket money
On the day's supply of gum –
Sometimes Kenny felt quite glum.
As he grew, so did his need –
There seemed no limit to his greed:
At ten he often put away
Ninety seven packs a day.

Then at last he went too far –
Sitting in his father's car,
Stuffing gum without a pause,
Found that he had jammed his jaws.
He nudged his dad and pointed to
The mouthful that he couldn't chew.
'Well, spit it out if you can't chew it!'
Ken shook his head. He couldn't do it.
Before long he began to groan –
The gum was solid as a stone.
Dad took him to a builder's yard;
They couldn't help. It was too hard.
They called a doctor and he said,
'This silly boy will soon be dead.
His mouth's so full of bubble-gum
No nourishment can reach his tum.'

Remember Ken and please do not
Go buying too much you-know-what.

Wendy Cope

THE CRUEL NAUGHTY BOY

There was a cruel naughty boy,
  Who sat upon the shore,
A-catching little fishes by
  The dozen and the score.

And as they squirmed and wriggled there,
  He shouted loud with glee,
'You surely cannot want to live,
  You're little-er than me.'

Just then with a malicious leer,
　　And a capacious smile,
Before him from the water deep
　　There rose a crocodile.

He eyed the little naughty boy,
　　Then heaved a blubbering sigh,
And said, 'You cannot want to live,
　　You're little-er than I.'

The fishes squirm and wriggle still,
　　Beside that sandy shore,
The cruel little naughty boy,
　　Was never heard of more.

William Cole

FLORADORA DOE

Consider the calamity
of Floradora Doe,
who talked to all her plants, because
she thought it helped them grow,
she recited to her ivy,
to her fennel, ferns, and phlox,
she chatted with her cacti
in their little window box.

She murmured to her mosses,
and she yammered to her yew,
she babbled to her basil,
to her borage and bamboo,
she lectured to her laurels,
to her lilac and her lime,
she whispered to her willows,
and she tittered to her thyme.

She gossiped with a poppy,
and she prattled to a rose,
she regaled her rhododendrons
with a constant stream of prose,
then suddenly, one morning,
every plant keeled over, dead.
'Alas!' moaned Floradora.
'Was it something that I said?'

Jack Prelutsky

THE RUBBER PLANT SPEAKS

Mostly they ignore me,
The white plants who walk.
Or bring me water in their leaves.

I wonder how they feed?
With their stubby roots?
And is their green beneath their skins?

Sometimes they talk to me,
But never listen.
They do not recognize my voice.

No one hears. No one hears.
No, not even him,
The little orange plant that swims.

Jan Dean

MAFIA CATS

We're the Mafia cats
   Bugsy, Franco and Toni
We're crazy for pizza
   With hot pepperoni

We run all the rackets
   From gambling to vice
On St Valentine's Day
   We massacre mice

We always wear shades
   To show that we're meanies
Big hats and sharp suits
   And drive Lamborghinis

We're the Mafia cats
   Bugsy, Franco and Toni
Love Sicilian wine
   And cheese macaroni

But we have a secret
   (And if you dare tell
You'll end up with the kitten
   At the bottom of the well

Or covered in concrete
   And thrown into the deep
For this is one secret
   You really must keep).

We're the Cosa Nostra
   Run the scams and the fiddles
But at home we are
   Mopsy, Ginger and Tiddles.

(Breathe one word and you're cat-meat. OK?)

Roger McGough

THE TIGER

A tiger going for a stroll
Met an old man and ate him whole.

The old man shouted, and he thumped.
The tiger's stomach churned and bumped.

The other tigers said: 'Now really,
We hear your breakfast much too clearly.'

The moral is, he should have chewed.
It does no good to bolt one's food.

Edward Lucie-Smith

A LADY BORN UNDER A CURSE

A lady born under a curse
Used to drive forth each day in a hearse;
   From the back she would wail
   Through a thickness of veil
'Things do not get better but worse.'

Edward Gorey

THE PRETTY YOUNG THING

A pretty young thing from St Paul's
Wore a newspaper gown to a ball.
   The dress caught on fire
   And burned her attire
Front page, sporting section and all.

Anonymous

WHAT'S THE MATTER UP THERE?

'What's the matter up there?'
'Playing soldiers.'
'But soldiers don't make that kind of noise.'
'We're playing the kind of soldier that
makes that kind of noise.'

Carl Sandburg

LO! THE DRUM-MAJOR

Lo! the drum-major in his coat of gold,
His blazing breeches and high-towering cap –
Imperiously pompous, grandly bold,
Grim, resolute, an awe-inspiring chap!
Who'd think this gorgeous creature's only virtue
Is that in battle he will never hurt you?

Ambrose Bierce

UNCLE JAMES

My uncle James
Was a terrible man.
He cooked his wife
In the frying pan.

'She's far too tender
To bake or boil!'
He cooked her up
In peanut oil.

But sometime later –
A month or more –
There came a knock
On my uncle's door.

A great green devil
Was standing there.
He caught my uncle
By the hair.

'Are you the uncle
That cooked his wife,
And leads such a terribly
Wicked life?'

My uncle yowled
Like an old tom cat,
But the devil took him
For all of that.

Oh, take a tip
From my Uncle James!
Don't throw stones
And don't call names.

Just be as good
As ever you can –
And never cook aunts
In a frying pan!

Margaret Mahy

DON'T-CARE

Don't-care didn't care;
   Don't-care was wild.
Don't-care stole plum and pear
   Like any beggar's child.

Don't-care was made to care,
   Don't-care was hung:
Don't-care was put in the pot
   And boiled till he was done.

Anonymous

MATILDA
Who told Lies, and was Burned to Death

Matilda told such Dreadful Lies,
It made one Gasp and Stretch one's Eyes;
Her Aunt, who, from her Earliest Youth,
Had kept a Strict Regard for Truth,
Attempted to Believe Matilda:
The effort very nearly killed her,
And would have done so, had not She
Discovered this Infirmity.
For once, towards the Close of Day,
Matilda, growing tired of play,
And finding she was left alone,
Went tiptoe to the Telephone
And summoned the Immediate Aid
Of London's Noble Fire-Brigade.
Within an hour the Gallant Band
Were pouring in on every hand,
From Putney, Hackney Downs and Bow,
With Courage high and Hearts a-glow
They galloped, roaring through the Town,
'Matilda's House is Burning Down!'
Inspired by British Cheers and Loud
Proceeding from the Frenzied Crowd,
They ran their ladders through a score
Of windows on the Ball Room Floor;
And took Peculiar Pains to Souse
The Pictures up and down the House,
Until Matilda's Aunt succeeded
In showing them they were not needed
And even then she had to pay
To get the Men to go away!

It happened that a few Weeks later
Her Aunt was off to the Theatre
To see that Interesting Play
The Second Mrs. Tanqueray.
She had refused to take her Niece
To hear this Entertaining Piece:
A Deprivation Just and Wise
To Punish her for Telling Lies.
That Night a Fire *did* break out—
You should have heard Matilda Shout!
You should have heard her Scream and Bawl,
And throw the window up and call
To People passing in the Street—
(The rapidly increasing Heat
Encouraging her to obtain
Their confidence)—but all in vain!
For every time She shouted 'Fire!'
They only answered 'Little Liar!'
And therefore when her Aunt returned,
Matilda, and the House, were Burned.

Hilaire Belloc

TV

In the house
of Mr and Mrs Spouse
he and she
would watch TV
and never a word
between them spoken
until the day
the set was broken.

Then 'How do you do?'
said he to she,
'I don't believe
that we've met yet.
Spouse is my name.
What's yours?' he asked.

'Why, mine's the same!'
said she to he,
'Do you suppose that we could be – ?'

But the set came suddenly right about,
and so they never did find out.

Eve Merriam

THE PYTHON

A Python I should not advise, –
It needs a doctor for its eyes,
And has the measles yearly.

However, if you feel inclined
To get one (to improve your mind,
And not from fashion merely),

Allow no music near its cage;
And when it flies into a rage
Chastise it, most severely.

I had an aunt in Yucatan
Who bought a Python from a man
And kept it for a pet.

She died, because she never knew
These simple little rules and few; –
The Snake is living yet.

Hilaire Belloc

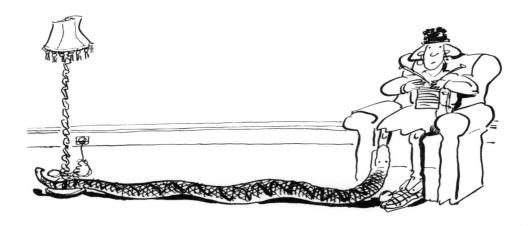

THAT'LL BE ALL RIGHT YOU'LL FIND

James has hated motorists ever since the day
They ran him down and broke his legs in such a heartless
way;
   Oh, My! There are some careless men!
   But what was worse than that was when
   Poor Jimmy heard him say:
   'That'll be all right you'll find!
   That'll be all right you'll find!
   No more trousers! No more boots!
   Only coat and waistcoat suits
   That'll be all right you'll find!
   You'll walk upon your hands instead
   And have more time to use your head,
   That'll be all right you'll find!'

Mabel fainted right away, they thought that she was dead;
The dentist was shortsighted – pulled her nose clean off her
head!
   Oh My! There are some careless men,
   But what was worse than that was when
   He turned to her and said:
   'That'll be all right you'll find!
   That'll be all right you'll find!
   It was a neat extraction, that,
   And now you'd best put on your hat,
   That'll be all right you'll find!
   No more horrid colds and sniffs!
   No more dirty handkerchiefs!
   That'll be all right you'll find!'

   Rum-Tarrarra! Pom! Pom!

L. de Giberne Sieveking

85

QUIET FUN

My son Augustus, in the street, one day,
   Was feeling quite exceptionally merry.
A stranger asked him: 'Can you show me, pray,
   The quickest way to Brompton Cemetery?'
'The quickest way? You bet I can!' said Gus,
And pushed the fellow underneath a bus.

Whatever people say about my son,
He does enjoy his little bit of fun.

Harry Graham

OUR DOGGY

First he sat, and then he lay,
And then he said: I've come to stay.
And that is how we acquired our doggy Pontz.
He is all right as dogs go, but not quite what one wants.
Because he talks. He talks like you and me.
And he is not you and me, he is made differently.
You think it is nice to have a talking animal?
It is not nice. It is unnatural.

Stevie Smith

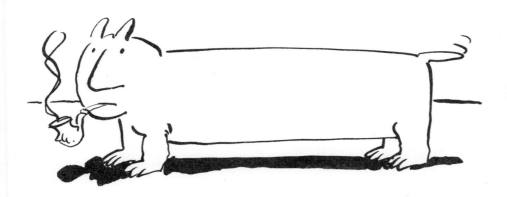

ADVICE TO CHILDREN

Caterpillars living on lettuce
Are the colour of their host:
Look out, when you're eating a salad,
For the greens that move the most.

Close your mouth tight when you're running
As when washing you shut your eyes,
Then as soap is kept from smarting
So will tonsils be from flies.

If in spite of such precautions
Anything nasty gets within,
Remember it will be thinking:
'Far worse for me than him.'

Roy Fuller

THE ITCH

If your hands get wet
in the washing-up water,
if they get covered in flour,
if you get grease or oil
all over your fingers,
if they land up in the mud,
wet grit, paint, or glue . . .

have you noticed
it's just then
that you always get
a terrible itch
just inside your nose?
And you can try to
twitch your nose,
twist your nose,
squeeze your nose,
scratch it with your arm,
scrape your nose on
your shoulder
or press it
up against the wall,
but it's no good.
You can't get rid of
the itch.
It drives you so mad
you just have to let a
finger get at it.
And before you know
you've done it.
you've wiped a load of glue,
or oil,
or cold wet pastry
all over the end of your nose.

Michael Rosen

89

ADVICE TO GROWN UPS AND OTHER ANIMALS......

(Written on a frog by Eric who ate too many worms and died.)

Be very careful
When you're swimming in the sink,
Cos the currents round the plughole,
Are stronger than you think.

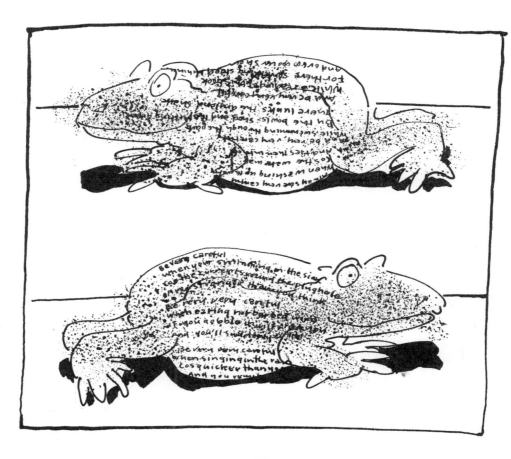

Be very, very careful
When you're eating hot barbed wire,
If you gobble, it will prick you,
And you'll suddenly expire.

Be very, very careful
When singing in the rain,
Cos quicker than you think, your clothes will shrink
And you won't get them off again.

Always be very careful
When washing up the pots,
Cos the water makes your fingers soft
And ties them into knots.

And be very, very careful
While swimming through the park,
By the bowls shed and the putting green
There lurks the Dry-Land Shark.

And be very, very careful
While a reading of this book,
For there's something stood behind you
And over your shoulder it looks......

Mike Harding

MY OBNOXIOUS BROTHER

My obnoxious brother Bobby
Has a most revolting hobby;
There, behind the garden wall is
Where he captures creepy-crawlies.

Grannies, aunts and baby cousins
Come to our house in their dozens,
But they disappear discreetly
When they see him smiling sweetly.

For they know, as he approaches,
In his pockets are cockroaches,
Spiders, centipedes and suchlike;
All of which they do not much like.

As they head towards the lobby,
Bidding fond farewells to Bobby,
How they wish he'd change his habits
And keep guinea pigs or rabbits.

But their wishes are quite futile,
For he thinks that bugs are cute. I'll
Finish now, but just remind you:
Bobby could be right behind you!

Colin West

MY LAST NATURE WALK

I strode among the clumihacken
Where scrubble nudges to the barfter
Till I whumped into, hidden in the bracken,
A groolted after-laughter-rafter.

(For milty Wah-Zohs do guffaw
Upon a laughter-rafter perch.
But after laughter they balore
Unto a second beam to gurch.)

Yet here was but one gollamonce!
I glumped upon the after-laughter-rafter.
Where was its other-brother? Oh! My bonce!
The Wah-Zohs blammed it with a laughter-rafter.

    Moral: Never gamble on a bramble ramble.

Adrian Mitchell

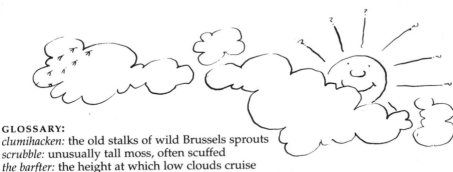

GLOSSARY:
clumihacken: the old stalks of wild Brussels sprouts
scrubble: unusually tall moss, often scuffed
the barfter: the height at which low clouds cruise
to whump: to bump into, winding oneself in the process
groolted: cunningly engraved with the portraits of little-known and famous barbers
milty: clean but mean-minded
Wah-Zohs: French birds, sometimes spelt Oiseaux
to balore: to hover fatly downwards
to gurch: to recover from cheerfulness
gollamonce: a thing that is sought for desperately, although there is no good reason for finding it
to glump: to glump
to blam: to shonk on the cloddle

93

THE FRIENDLY CINNAMON BUN

Shining in his stickiness and glistening with honey,
Safe among his sisters and his brothers on a tray,
With raisin eyes that looked at me as I put down my money,
There smiled a friendly cinnamon bun, and
　　this I heard him say:

'It's a lovely, lovely morning, and the world's a
　　lovely place;
I know it's going to be a lovely day.
I know we're going to be good friends; I like
　　your honest face;
Together we might go a long, long way.'

The baker's girl rang up the sale, 'I'll wrap your
　　bun,' said she.
'Oh no, you needn't bother,' I replied.
I smiled back at that cinnamon bun and ate
　　him, one two three,
And walked out with his friendliness inside.

Russell Hoban

FUNNY HONEY

You're my honey.
You're my sweet.
You're my pumpkin
Pie to eat.
You're my ice cream.
You're my ices.
You're my seasoning
And spices.
You're my candy.
You're my cake.
Oops! I ate you
By mistake!

Douglas Florian

I'D LIKE TO BE A TEABAG

I'd like to be a teabag,
And stay at home all day –
And talk to other teabags
In a teabag sort of way . . .

I'd love to be a teabag,
And lie in a little box –
And never have to wash my face
Or change my dirty socks . . .

I'd like to be a teabag,
An Earl Grey one perhaps,
And doze all day and lie around
With Earl Grey kind of chaps.

I wouldn't have to do a thing,
No homework, jobs or chores –
Comfy in my caddy
Of teabags and their snores.

I wouldn't have to do exams,
I needn't tidy rooms,
Or sweep the floor or feed the cat
Or wash up all the spoons.

I wouldn't have to do a thing,
A life of bliss – you see . . .
Except that once in all my life

I'd make a cup of tea!

Peter Dixon

RATTLESNAKE MEAT

A gourmet challenged me to eat
A tiny bit of rattlesnake meat,
Remarking, 'Don't look horror-stricken,
You'll find it tastes a lot like chicken.'
It did.
Now chicken I cannot eat
Because it tastes like rattlesnake meat.

Ogden Nash

RHINOCEROS STEW

If you want to make a rhinoceros stew
all in the world that you have to do
is skin a rhinoceros, cut it in two
and stew it and stew it and stew it.

When it's stewed so long that you've quite forgot
what it is that's bubbling in the pot
dish it up promptly, serve it hot
and chew it and chew it and chew it

and chew it and chew it and chew it
and chew it and chew it and chew it.

AND CHEW IT AND CHEW IT AND CHEW IT

Mildred Luton

VEGETARIANS

Vegetarians are cruel unthinking people.
Everybody knows that a carrot screams when grated
That a peach bleeds when torn apart.
Do you believe an orange insensitive
to thumbs gouging out its flesh?
That tomatoes spill their brains
painlessly? Potatoes, skinned alive
and boiled, the soil's little lobsters.
Don't tell me it doesn't hurt
when peas are ripped from their overcoats,
the hide flayed off sprouts,
cabbage shredded, onions beheaded.

Throw in the trowel and lay down the hoe.
Mow no more. Let my people go!

Roger McGough

99

BANANAS

They have made the colour yellow
famous for its shape.

I like the way their skins unzip
and are vital, in cartoon strips
for unfooting the escapes
of innocent villains.

Their word is a friendly name
for madness.

They have no pips and thus
may be chewed without indignity
or teeth.

They give the sedate fruitbowl
its brazen smile.

Brian McCabe

THE PRUNE

Some base their claims
On tang alone,
But I admire a fruit
That does a job.

Robert Shure

THE HARDEST THING TO DO IN THE WORLD

is stand in the hot sun
at the end of a long queue for ice creams
watching all the people who've just bought theirs
coming away from the queue
giving their ice creams their very first lick.

Michael Rosen

MASHED POTATO/LOVE POEM

If I ever had to choose between you
and a third helping of mashed potato,
(whipped lightly with a fork
not whisked,
and a little pool of butter
melting in the middle . . .)

I think
I'd choose
the mashed potato.

But I'd choose you next.

Sidney Hoddes

IF YOU'RE NO GOOD AT COOKING

If you're no good at cooking,
Can't fry or bake,

Here's something you
Can always make. Take

Three very ordinary
Slices of bread:

Stack the second
On the first one's head.

Stack the third
On top of that.

There! Your three slices
Lying pat.

So what have you got?
A BREAD SANDWICH,

That's what!
Why not?

Kit Wright

GREEDYGUTS

I sat in the café and sipped at a Coke.
There sat down beside me a WHOPPING great bloke
Who sighed as he elbowed me into the wall:
'Your trouble, my boy, is your belly's too small!
Your bottom's too thin! Take a lesson from me:
I may not be nice, but I'm great, you'll agree,
And I've lasted a lifetime by playing this hunch:
The bigger the breakfast, the larger the lunch!

The larger the lunch, then the huger the supper.
The deeper the teapot, the vaster the cupper.
The fatter the sausage, the fuller the tea.
The MORE on the table, the BETTER FOR ME!'

His elbows moved in and his elbows moved out,
His belly grew bigger, chins wobbled about,
As forkful by forkful and plate after plate,
He ate and he ate and he ate and he ATE!

I hardly could breathe, I was squashed out of shape,
So under the table I made my escape.
'Aha!' he rejoiced, 'when it's put to the test,
The fellow who's fattest will come off the best!
Remember, my boy, when it comes to the crunch:
The bigger the breakfast, the larger the lunch!

The larger the lunch, then the huger the supper.
The deeper the teapot, the vaster the cupper.
The fatter the sausage, the fuller the tea.
The MORE on the table, the BETTER FOR ME!'

A lady came by who was scrubbing the floor
With a mop and a bucket. To even the score,
I lifted that bucket of water and said,
As I poured the whole lot of it over his head:

'I've found all my life, it's a pretty sure bet:
The FULLER the bucket, the WETTER YOU GET!'

Kit Wright

I'D RATHER BE A SAUSAGE

I'd rather be a sausage
Than a British Man of War,
Or a Caterpillar with a broken arm.
Corduroy braces are all very well,
And give no immediate cause for alarm.
But the sausage is a mighty beast,
Who serves only to please.
In fact, he is the mightiest there is.
Content to lie in frying pans
For ages at a stretch
Singing Sizzle Sizzle Sizzle Sizzle Sizz!

Billy Connolly

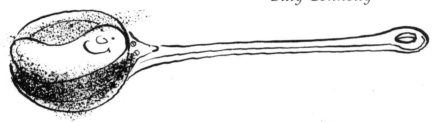

COCKROACH SANDWICH

Cockroach sandwich
For my lunch,
Hate the taste
But love the crunch!

Colin McNaughton

UNTITLED

At my birthday party
I had chocolate cake,
And cheesecake,
And fruitcake,
And ginger cake,
And fudge cake.
After that I had stummer cake.

Anthony Browne

LIKE A BEACON

In London
every now and then
I get this craving
for my mother's food
I leave art galleries
in search of plantains
saltfish/sweet potatoes

I need this link

I need this touch
of home
swinging my bag
like a beacon
against the cold

Grace Nichols

UNCLE ED'S HEADS

Fame was a claim of Uncle Ed's,
Simply because he had three heads,
Which, if he'd only had a third of,
I think he would never have been heard of.

Ogden Nash

MARVO

Marvo the Magician
said, 'Young man, come over here
please put this coin inside your hand
and I'll make it disappear.'
He did.
And the one handed young man went home.

David Wood

EASY MONEY

Guess how old I am?
I bet you can't.
I bet you.
Go on guess.
Have a guess.

Wrong!
Have another.

Wrong!
Have another

Wrong again!
Do you give in?

Seven years four months two weeks
five days three hours fifteen
minutes forty-eight seconds!
That's 50 cents you owe me.

Roger McGough

THIS IS THE HAND

This is the hand
that touched the frost
that froze my tongue
and made it numb

this is the hand
that cracked the nut
that went in my mouth
and never came out

this is the hand
that slid round the bath
to find the soap
that wouldn't float

this is the hand
on the hot water bottle
meant to warm my bed
that got lost instead

this is the hand
that held the bottle
that let go of the soap
that cracked the nut
that touched the frost
this is the hand
that never gets lost.

Michael Rosen

FIVE LITTLE BROTHERS

5 little brothers set out together
   To journey the livelong day,
In a curious carriage all made of leather
   They hurried away, away!
One big brother, and 3 quite small,
And one wee fellow, no size at all.

The carriage was dark and none too roomy,
And they could not move about;
The 5 little brothers grew very gloomy,
And the wee one began to pout,
Till the biggest one whispered: 'What
                    do you say?
Let's leave the carriage and run away!'

So out they scampered, the 5 together,
And off and away they sped;
When somebody found the carriage of leather,
Oh my, how she shook her head!
Twas her little boy's shoe, as
                    everyone knows,
And the 5 little brothers were 5
                    little toes.

Anonymous

LOST CONTACT

O the vexation
of dropping
a contact lens!

The contact lens
that would help you find
the contact lens
you are looking for
is
the contact lens
you are looking for!

William Cole

I
NEED
CONTACT
L   E   N   S   E   S

like I need a poke in the eye

John Hegley

A BLINK

A blink, I think, is the same as a wink,
A blink is a wink that grew,
For a *wink* you wink with only one eye,
And a *blink* you wink with two!

Jacqueline Segal

WINK

I took 40 winks
yesterday afternoon
and another 40 today.
In fact I get through
about 280 winks a week.
Which is about 14,560
winks a year.
(The way I'm going on
I'll end up looking like a wink)

Roger McGough

LIMBO DANCER'S SOUNDPOEM

Go
down
low
     low
show   low
dem
what
you know
         know
let   know
limb
flow
     flow
         flow
as sound
of drum
grow
     grow
         grow
& body
bend
like bow
     bow
         bow
            limb/bow
              low
                low
                  low
                    limb/bow

John Agard

OH TO BE

Oh to be a broken leg
In plaster white as chalk
And travel everywhere by crutch
While others have to walk.

Mike Griffin

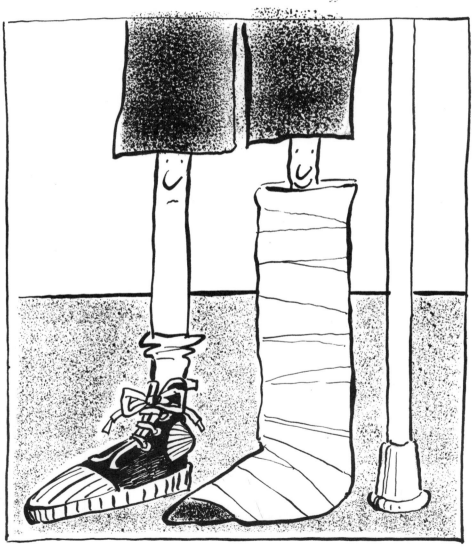

WHEN TO CUT YOUR FINGERNAILS

Cut them on Monday
There's a good week ahead

Cut them on Tuesday
Better go straight to bed

Cut them on Wednesday
You're going to be rich

Cut them on Thursday
You might meet a witch

Cut them on Friday
You'll be walked off your feet

Cut them on Saturday
You're in for a treat

But cut them on Sunday
Without saying a prayer
And your nails will grow
As long as your hair!

Roger McGough

MARIGOLDS

I bought a bottle of Nettle Shampoo
this morning.
When I got home I wondered whether
I shouldn't shampoo
the marigolds
as well.

Adrian Henri

NORMAN NORTON'S NOSTRILS

Oh, Norman Norton's nostrils
are powerful and strong;
Hold on to your belongings
If he should come along.

And do not ever let him
Inhale with all this might,
Or else your pens and pencils
Will disappear from sight.

Right up his nose they'll vanish
Your future will be black.
Unless he gets the sneezes
You'll *never* get them back.

Colin West

THE SNIFFLE

In spite of her sniffle
Isabel's chiffle.
Some girls with a sniffle
Would be weepy and tiffle;
They would look awful,
Like a rained-on waffle,
But Isabel's chiffle
In spite of her sniffle.
Her nose is more red
With a cold in her head,
But then, to be sure,
Her eyes are bluer.
Some girls with a snuffle,
Their tempers are uffle.
But when Isabel's snivelly
She's snivelly civilly,
And when she's snuffly
She's perfectly luffly.

Ogden Nash

121

THE SNIFFLE

A sniffle crouches on the terrace
in wait for someone he can harass.

And suddenly he jumps with vim
upon a man by name of Schrimm.

Paul Schrimm, responding with 'hatchoo,'
is stuck with him the weekend through.

Christian Morgenstern

JOB SATISFACTION

I am a young bacterium
And I enjoy my work
I snuggle into people's food
I lie in wait – I lurk.
They chomp a bit and chew a bit
And say, 'This can't be beaten'
But then in bed they groan and moan,
'I wish I hadn't eaten.'

John Collis

THE BATTLE

Not Alamein or Waterloo:
   The battlefield's my throat!
The enemy, a savage horde
   That swarms across the moat
And storms the citadel –
While the defence is sleeping well.

The white cells then – my bodyguard –
   Join battle with the germs;
Kill millions, but, in turn, are killed;
   The rest are offered terms –
Then, backed by millions more,
Fight on . . . the field, meanwhile, is sore.

At last, with penicillin's aid,
   My throat's at peace again.
Earth, you were sore at Waterloo,
   Hastings and Alamein,
And still have little ease:
Invent your penicillin, please!

Edward Lowbury

NIGHT STARVATION OR THE BITER BIT

At night my Uncle Rufus
(Or so I've heard it said)
Would put his teeth into a glass
Of water by his bed.

At three o'clock one morning
He woke up with a cough,
And as he reached out for his teeth –
They bit his hand right off.

Carey Blyton

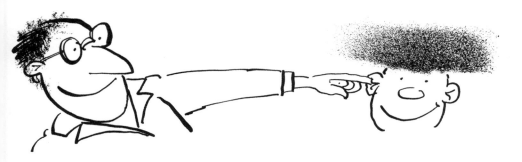

INTELLIGENCE TEST

'What do you use your eyes for?'
The white-coated man enquired.
'I use my eyes for looking,'
Said Toby, '– unless I'm tired.'

'I see. And then you close them,'
Observed the white-coated man.
'Well done. A very good answer.
Let's try another one.

'What is your nose designed for?
What use is the thing to you?'
'I use my nose for smelling,'
Said Toby, 'don't you, too?'

'I do indeed,' said the expert,
'That's what the thing is for.
Now I've another question to ask you,
Then there won't be any more.

'What are your ears intended for?
Those things at each side of your head?
Come on – don't be shy – I'm sure you can say.'
'For washing behind,' Toby said.

Vernon Scannell

EARS

Have you thought to give three cheers
For the usefulness of ears?
Ears will often spring surprises
Coming in such different sizes.
Ears are crinkled, even folded.
Ears turn pink when you are scolded.
Ears can have the oddest habits
Standing rather straight on rabbits.
Ears are little tape-recorders
Catching all the family orders.
Words, according to your mother,
Go in one and out the other.
Each side of your head you'll find them.
Don't forget to wash behind them.
Precious little thanks they'll earn you
Hearing things that don't concern you.

Max Fatchen

PUT THAT RABBIT DOWN AND COME AND EAT YOUR DINNER

A HANDSOME YOUNG FELLOW CALLED FREARS

A handsome young fellow called Frears
Was attracted to girls by their ears.
He'd traverse the globe
For a really nice lobe,
And the sight would reduce him to tears.

Michael Palin

GIVE UP SLIMMING, MUM

My Mum
is short
and plump
and pretty
and I wish
she'd give up
slimming.

So does Dad.

Her cooking's
delicious –
you can't
beat it –
but you really can
hardly bear
to eat it –
the way she sits
with her eyes
brimming,

watching you
polish off
the spuds
and trimmings
while she
has nothing
herself but a small
thin dry
diet biscuit:
that's all.

My Mum
is short
and plump
and pretty
and I wish
she'd give up
slimming.

So does Dad.

She says she
looks as though
someone had
sat on her –
BUT WE LIKE MUM
WITH A BIT
OF FAT ON HER!

Kit Wright

. . . AND A FAT POEM

Fat is
as fat is
as fat is

Fat does
as fat thinks

Fat feels
as fat please

Fat believes

        Fat is to butter
        as milk is to cream
        fat is to sugar
        as pud is to steam

Fat is a dream
in times of lean

        fat is a darling
        a dumpling
        a squeeze
        fat is cuddles
        up a baby's sleeve

        and fat speaks for itself

Grace Nichols

HUSBANDS AND WIVES

Husbands and wives
   With children between them
Sit in the subway;
   So I have seen them.

One word only
   From station to station;
So much talk for
   So close a relation.

Miriam Hershenson

THE PARENT

Children aren't happy with nothing to ignore,
And that's what parents were created for.

Ogden Nash

UNCLE FUDGE TOLD LIES

My Uncle Fudge told lies!
Was a deep sea diver once he said,
Kicked fishes and chips on the ocean bed
Played gin rummy and snap with an octoped
For a stake of chocolate mice.

My Uncle Fudge told fibs!
Said he sailed the main with Captain Hook
When the food got bad they keel-hauled the cook,
They said 'The burned jelly fish we could overlook
But you singed Sid Kidd's squid you did.'

My Uncle Fudge told whoppers!
Said he was swallowed by a whale on Blackpool shore
And lived in its innards for twelve month or more
And on long afternoons to stop himself getting bored
He scrubbed the old Leviathan's choppers!

My Uncle Fudge tergiversated!
Said he could eat worms without going mad,
Said he'd done so since he was a lad,
Said with butterfly sauce they didn't taste bad
And he'd eat them until he was sated! . . .

My Uncle Fudge told untruths!
Said that when that he had been a youth
He'd fought with an uncouth wiffenpoof
That had gnawed a big hole in his grandad's roof
So he'd knocked out one of its tooths!

My Uncle Fudge told stretchers!
Said he'd once been marooned in the Sahara
With only a jar of cascara
And an onyx and ormolu candelabra
Did we disbelieve him . . . you betchas.

My Uncle Fudge he lied!
Said he would live till the end of time,
Till three hundred thousand zillion and seventy nine!
And how did I know in the end he was lying
Last Wednesday at tea
He choked on a pea
And said 'O.K. I own up'
And died.

Mike Harding

CHRISTMAS THANK YOU'S

Dear Auntie
Oh, what a nice jumper
I've always adored powder blue
and fancy you thinking of
orange and pink
for the stripes
how clever of you

Dear Uncle
The soap is
terrific
So
useful
and such a kind thought and
how did you guess that
I'd just used the last of
the soap that last Christmas brought

Dear Gran
Many thanks for the hankies
Now I really can't wait for the flu
and the daisies embroidered
in red round the 'M'
for Michael
how
thoughtful of you

Dear Cousin
What socks!
and the same sort you wear
so you must be
the last word in style
and I'm certain you're right that the
luminous green
will make me stand out a mile

Dear Sister
I quite understand your concern
it's a risk sending jam in the post
But I think I've pulled out
all the big bits
of glass
so it won't taste too sharp
spread on toast

Dear Grandad
Don't fret
I'm delighted
So *don't* think your gift will
offend
I'm not at all hurt
that you gave up this year
and just sent me
a fiver
to spend

Mick Gowar

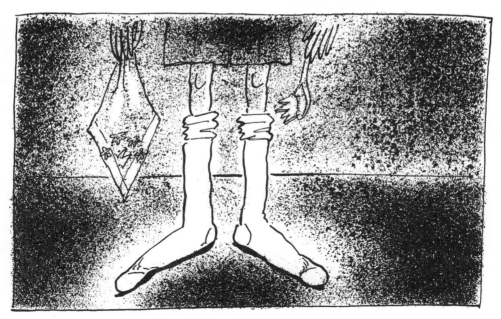

SISTERS

If only I hadn't had sisters
How much more romantic I'd be
But my sisters were such little blisters
That all women are sisters to me.

Anonymous

MY SISTER LAURA

My sister Laura's bigger than me
And lifts me up quite easily.
I can't lift her, I've tried and tried;
She must have something heavy inside.

Spike Milligan

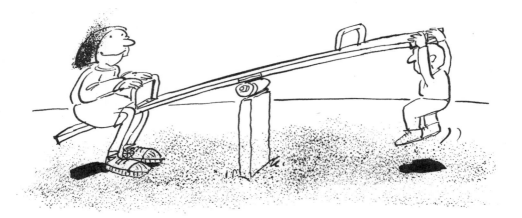

EXACTLY LIKE A 'V'

When my brother Tommy

Sleeps in bed with me

He doubles up

And makes

himself

exactly

like

a

V

And 'cause the bed is not so wide
A part of him is on my side.

Abram Bunn Ross

SQUEEZES

We love to squeeze bananas,
We love to squeeze ripe plums,
And when they are feeling sad
We love to squeeze our mums.

Brian Patten

I WONDER WHY DAD IS SO THOROUGHLY MAD

I wonder why Dad is so thoroughly mad,
I can't understand it at all,
unless it's the bee still afloat in his tea,
or his underwear, pinned to the wall.

Perhaps it's the dye on his favorite tie,
or the mousetrap that snapped in his shoe,
or the pipeful of gum that he found with his thumb,
or the toilet, sealed tightly with glue.

It can't be the bread crumbled up in his bed,
or the slugs someone left in the hall,
I wonder why Dad is so thoroughly mad,
I can't understand it at all.

Jack Prelutsky

MY DAD, YOUR DAD

My dad's fatter than your dad,
Yes, my dad's fatter than yours:
If he eats any more he won't fit in the house,
He'll have to live out of doors.

Yes, but my dad's balder than your dad,
My dad's balder, O.K.,
He's only got two hairs left on his head
And both are turning grey.

Ah, but my dad's thicker than your dad,
My dad's thicker, all right.
He has to look at his watch to see
If it's noon or the middle of the night.

Yes, but my dad's more boring than your dad.
If he ever starts counting sheep
When he can't get to sleep at night, he finds
It's the sheep that go to sleep.

But my dad doesn't mind your dad.
Mine quite likes yours too.
I suppose they don't always think much of us!
That's true, I suppose, that's true.

Kit Wright

LAURIE AND DORRIE

The first thing that you'll notice if
   You meet my Uncle Laurie
Is how, whatever else he does,
   He can't stop saying sorry.

He springs from bed at 5 a.m.
   As birds begin to waken,
Cries, 'No offence intended lads –
   Likewise, I hope, none taken!'

This drives his wife, my Auntie Dorrie,
   Mad. It's not surprising
She grabs him by the throat and screeches,
   'Stop apologizing!'

My Uncle, who's a little deaf,
   Says, 'Sorry? Sorry, Dorrie?'
'For goodness' sake,' Aunt Dorrie screams,
   'Stop saying sorry, Laurie!'

'Sorry, dear? Stop saying what?'
   'SORRY!' Laurie's shaken.
'No need to be, my dear,' he says,
   For *no offence is taken.*

Likewise I'm sure that there was none
   Intended on your part.'
'Dear Lord,' Aunt Dorrie breathes, 'what can
   I do, where do I start?'

Then, 'Oh, I *see*,' says Uncle L.,
   'You mean "stop saying sorry"!
I'm sorry to have caused offence –
   Oops! Er . . . *sorry*, Dorrie!'

Kit Wright

CAR ATTACK

On last year's Halloween
A car hit Auntie Jean.
Unhinged by this attack,
My Auntie hit it back.

She hit it with her handbag
And knocked it with her knee.
She socked it with a sandbag
And thumped it with a tree.

On last year's Halloween
A car hit Auntie Jean.
And now, my Auntie's better
But the car is with the wrecker.

Doug Macleod

COUSIN NELL

Cousin Nell
married a frogman
in the hope
that one day
he would turn into
a handsome prince.

Instead he turned into
a sewage pipe
near Gravesend
and was never seen again.

Roger McGough

AUNT ERMINTRUDE

Aunt Ermintrude
was determined to
swim across the Channel.
Each week she'd
practise in the bath
encostumed in flannel.

The tap end
was Cap Gris Nez
the slippy slopes
were Dover. She'd
doggypaddle up and down
vaselined all over.

After 18 months, Aunt Erm was in peak condition.
So, one cold grey morning in March
she boarded the Channel steamer at Dover
went straight to her cabin
climbed into the bath
and urged on by a few well-wishers,
Aunt Ermintrude, completely nude
swam all the way to France.
Vive la tante!

Roger McGough

MY AUNT

I take my Aunt out in her pram
I am her grown-up Nephew 'Sam'!
My Grandma's sister married late
And by a stroke of Life's strange fate
Her children all arrived when we
Were roundabout aged Twenty-three.
It is most pleasing for a chap
To bounce his Aunt upon his lap!

Peggy Wood

UNCLE AND AUNTIE

My auntie gives me a colouring book and crayons.
I choose the picture of the puppies in a wicker basket.
I begin to colour.
After a while Auntie leans over to see what I have done
and says 'you've gone over the lines,
that's what you've done!
What do you think they're there for, eh?
Some kind of statement is it?
Going to be a rebel are we?
Your auntie's given you a nice present
and you've gone and spoilt it.'
I begin to cry.
My uncle gives me a hanky and some blank paper.
'Do some doggies of your own,' he says.
I begin to colour.
When I have done
he looks over
and says they are all very good.
He is lying;
only some of them are.

John Hegley

148

GRANDMA

My grandmother's a peaceful person, and she loves to sit.
But there never was a grandma who was such a one to knit.

> Scarves, caps, suits, socks –
> Her needles tick like fifty clocks
> But not for you and not for me.
> What makes her knit so busily?

All summer wasps toil tirelessly to earn their daily dinner,
Their black and yellow jerseys getting shabbier and thinner.

> Grandma knows just how a wasp grows
> Weary of its one suit of clothes.
> She knits flowered skirts and speckled pants –
> Now they can go to the beach or a dance.

Under the ice the goldfish hear December blizzards beating.
They have no fire at all down there, no rooms with central
heating.

> So when frost nips the lily roots
> Grandma's knitting woolly suits –
> Greens, blues, the goldfish adore them!
> Winter-long they're thankful for them.

When snowy winds are slicing in through all the little
crannies
The shrubs and birds in our neighbours' gardens envy those
in my granny's.

> Her shrubs have scarves and pullovers,
> Her birds have ear-muffs over their ears,
> And cats that come asking for 'Titbits please'
> Go trotting away with little bootees.

149

A frosty Octopus received a stout eight-fingered mitten.
A Camel whose important hump tended to get frost-bitten

Has a tea-cosy with tassels on it.
A grass-snake has a sock with a bonnet.
Folks can buy clothes at some shop or other.
The creatures depend on my grandmother.

Ted Hughes

THE UNDERWATER WIBBLES

The Underwater Wibbles
dine exclusively on cheese,
they keep it in containers
which they bind about their knees,
they often chew on Cheddar
which they slice into a dish,
and gorge on Gorgonzola
to the wonder of the fish.

The Underwater Wibbles
wiggle blithely through the sea,
munching merrily on Muenster,
grated Feta, bits of Brie,
passing porpoises seem puzzled,
stolid octopuses stare,
as the Wibbles nibble Gouda,
Provolone, Camembert.

The Underwater Wibbles
frolic gaily off the coast,
eating melted Mozzarella
served on soggy crusts of toast,
Wibbles gobble Appenzeller
as they execute their dives,
oh, the Underwater Wibbles
live extraordinary lives.

Jack Prelutsky

ONE MEAL TOO MANY

Samuel, the killer shark,
is feeling out of sorts –
he has a splitting headache
and his temper's rather short.

His nose is red and lumpy,
one fin is bent and torn,
his eyes are glazed and bloodshot
and he's feeling so forlorn.

He's in the Shark Infirmary,
he'll need to stay a week –
he tried to eat a submarine
and broke off all his teeth.

Patricia Leighton

JONAH AND THE WHALE

Well, to start with
It was dark
So dark
You couldn't see
Your hand in front of your face;
And huge
Huge as an acre of farmland.
How do I know?
Well, I paced it out
Length and breadth
That's how.
And if you was to shout
You'd hear your own voice resound,
Bouncing along the ridges of its stomach,
Like when you call out
Under a bridge
Or in an empty hall.
Hear anything?
No not much,
Only the normal
Kind of sounds
You'd expect to hear
Inside a whale's stomach;
The sea swishing far away,
Food gurgling, the wind
And suchlike sounds;
Then there was me screaming for help,
But who'd be likely to hear,
Us being miles from
Any shipping lines
And anyway

Supposing someone did hear,
Who'd think of looking inside a whale?
That's not the sort of thing
That people do.
Smell?
I'll say there was a smell.
And cold. The wind blew in
Something terrible from the South
Each time he opened his mouth
Or took a swallow of some tit bit.
The only way I found
To keep alive at all
Was to wrap my arms
Tight round myself
And race from wall to wall.
Damp? You can say that again;
When the ocean came sluicing in
I had to climb his ribs
To save myself from drowning.
Fibs? You think I'm telling you fibs,
I haven't told the half of it.
Brother
I'm only giving a modest account
Of what these two eyes have seen
And that's the truth on it.
Here, one thing I'll say
Before I'm done –
Catch me eating fish
From now on.

Gareth Owen

154

A SAIL ON THE SEA

A sail on the sea
Is a thing that suits me,
And I've done some sailing, it's true;
I've been at m' wits end
When sailing to Land's End
And one night – when I'd 'ad one or two –
The Captain came out on the bridge and said, 'Lads!
'We're all doomed . . .
'The 'ole tub's goin' down.
'To the boats. Every man. Except you.' I said,
    'Me?' He said,
'Yes, there's no room, you must drown.'
I said 'Drown?' He said, '*Drown*; the 'ole ship's
    goin' down,
'Don't stand arguin' there,
'I've just told you straight
'There's not room for you mate,
'On the boats or in fact anywhere.
'I know it's upsetting
'But what's the use of fretting?
'We might have lost all of the crew;
'But *now*, as I say,
'We can all get away,
'And only lose one, and that's you.'

Robb Wilton

WELL, HARDLY EVER

Never throw a brick at a drownin' man
Outside a grocery store –
Always throw him a bar a soap –
And he'll wash himself ashore.

Anonymous

FISH STORY

Father and I went fishin' today.
We caught four fish, but one got away.
One got away – it's such a bother.
One got away and one got father!

Douglas Florian

THE MYSTERIOUS SMIRKLE

Some say the Smirkle was a Smatterbug
And loved to smatterbug about,
But exactly what it was or did
We never did find out.

Was the Smirkle friendly?
Was it calm, meek and mild?
Or was it mean and nasty,
Belligerent and wild?

Did it live on cabbages,
Or did it live on Mars?
Was it made of chocolate drops,
Or formed by the light of stars?

It's one of Life's small mysteries
And gladly goes to show
There are still things left on the earth
That we will never know.

Brian Patten

TEN THINGS MUMS NEVER SAY

Keep your mouth open when you eat,
   then you'll be able to talk at the same time.

Jump down the stairs.
   It's quicker than walking.

Don't eat all your vegetables.
   You won't have enough room for your sweets.

It's too early for bed.
   Stay up and watch television.

Be rude to your teachers.
   It would be dishonest to be polite.

By all means walk on the furniture.
   It's already badly scratched.

Don't brush your teeth.
   They'll only get dirty again.

It's not your fault that your pocket money
   only lasts for a day.

Wipe your feet on the sofas.
   That's what they're there for.

I was far worse behaved than you
   when I was young.

Steve Turner

at the top.

then eat you

his back

ride upon

let you

he will

in a shop

see one

if you

allivator

Beware the

Roger McGough

THE UPS AND DOWNS OF THE ELEVATOR CAR

The elevator car in the elevator shaft,
Complained of the buzzer, complained of the draught.
It said it felt carsick as it rose and fell,
It said it had a headache from the ringing of the bell.

'There is spring in the air,' sighed the elevator car.
Said the elevator man, 'You are well-off where you are.'
The car paid no attention but it frowned an ugly frown

                    w h e n

            up   it

        going   should

    started   be

it   going

And   down.

Down flashed the signal, but up went the car.
The elevator man cried, 'You are going much too far!'
Said the elevator car, 'I'm doing no such thing.
I'm through with buzzers buzzing, I'm looking for the spring!'

Then the elevator man began to shout and call
And all the people came running through the hall.

The elevator man began to call and shout
'The car won't stop! Let me out! Let me out!'

On went the car past the penthouse door.
On went the car up one flight more.
On went the elevator till it came to the top.
On went the elevator, and it would not stop!

Right through the roof went the man and the car.
And nobody knows where the two of them are!
(Nobody knows but everyone cares,
Wearily, drearily climbing the stairs!)

Now on a summer evening when you see a shooting star
Fly through the air, perhaps it is – that elevator car!

Caroline D. Emerson

EMBRIONIC MEGASTARS

We can play reggae music, funk and skiffle too.
We prefer heavy metal but the classics sometimes do.
We're keen on Tamla-Motown, folk and soul,
But most of all, what we like
Is basic rock and roll.
We can play the monochord, the heptachord and flute,
We're OK on the saxophone and think the glockenspiel is
cute,
We really love the tuba, the balalaika and guitar
And our duets on the clavichord are bound to take us far.
We think castanets are smashing, harmonicas are fun,
And with the ocarina have only just begun.
We've mastered synthesizers, bassoons and violins
As well as hurdy-gurdies, pan-pipes and mandolins.
The tom-tom and the tabor, the trumpet and the drum
We learnt to play in between the tintinnabulum.
We want to form a pop group
And will when we're eleven,
But at the moment Tracey's eight
And I am only seven.

Brian Patten

THE CHARGE OF THE MOUSE BRIGADE

Half an inch, half an inch,
Half an inch onward,
Into Cat Valley
Rode the Six Hundred.

'Forward the Mouse Brigade!
Ravage their fleas!' he said.
'Capture the cheese!' he said.
Onward they thundered.

Claws to the right of them.
Claws to the left of them.
Claws to the front of them.
Pounces unnumbered.

Crash! – through the Catty flanks!
Shattered their fishy ranks!
Captured the Cheddar! thanks
To the Mouse Brigade!
Noble Six Hundred.

Bernard Stone

JUNGLE TIPS

(1) KILLER BEE

If you are bitten by a killer bee, bite it right back. A series of alkaline anti-bodies will be released which you may spit on to the wound, neutralising it. There is also the keen satisfaction of biting its furry little body in two.

(2) PIRANHAS

If you are wading across the Amazon, and a school of piranhas starts to take an interest, hum like mad whilst spilling a bottle of tomato ketchup across the river. They will imagine that you are another bleeding humming-bird, and will shun you as they cannot abide feathers stuck to their teeth.

Ivor Cutler

VYMURA: THE SHADE CARD POEM

Now artistic I aint, but I went to choose paint
'cos the state of the place made me sick.
I got a shade card, consumers-aid card, but it stayed hard to
   pick.
So I asked her advice as to what would look nice,
would blend in and not get on my wick.

She said 'our Vymura is super in Durer,
or see what you think of this new shade, Vlaminck.
But I see that you're choosy . . .
Picasso is newsy . . . that's greyish-greeny-bluesy . . .
Derain's all the rage . . .
that's hot-pink and Fauve-ish . . .
There's Monet . . . that's mauve-ish . . .
And Schwitters,
that's sort-of-a-*beige*.'

She said 'Fellow next door just sanded his floor
and rollered on Rouault and Rothko
His hall, och it's Pollock an' he
did his lounge in soft Hockney
with his cornice picked out in Kokoshka.'

'Now avoid the Van Gogh, you'll not get it off,
the Bonnard is bonny,
you'd be safe with matt Manet,
the Goya is *gorgeous*
or Chagall in eggshell,
but full-gloss Lautrec's sort of tacky.
So stick if you can to satin-finish Cezanne
or Constable . . . that's kind of khaki.
Or the Gainsborough green . . .
and I'd call it hooey to say Cimabue
would never tone in with Soutine.'

'If it looks a bit narrow when you splash on Pissarro
one-coat Magritte covers over.'
She said 'this Hitchens is a nice shade for kitchens
with some Ernst to connect 'em at other end of the spectrum,
Botticelli's lovely in the louvre.
She said 'If it was mine I'd do it Jim Dine . . .
don't think me elitist or snobby . . .
but Filipo Lippi'd
look awfy insipid,
especially in a large-ish lobby!'

Well, I did one wall Watteau, with the skirting Giotto,
and the door and the pelmet in Poussin.
The ceiling's de Kooning,
other walls all in Hals
and the whole place looks quite . . . cavalier,
with the woodwork in Corot –
but I think tomorrow
I'll flat-white it back to Vermeer.

Liz Lochhead

DEAR MAUREEN

Dear Maureen,
I am a lamp-post.
Every Saturday evening at five o'clock
three boys
wearing blue and white scarves
blue and white hats
waving their arms in the air
and shouting,
come my way.
Sometimes they kick me.
Sometimes they kiss me.
What should I do
to get them to make up their minds?
Yours bewilderedly,
Annie Onlight.

Michael Rosen

THE REVOLT OF THE LAMP POSTS

Last night I saw the lamp posts
That light up our back street
Wiggle, and then wriggle
And then, suddenly, they'd feet.

Then they all cleared off and left us,
The whole street in the dark,
So I left the house and followed,
There were millions in the park.

All the lamps from miles around
Had run away tonight,
They were dancing, they were singing,
And they held each other tight.

The king, a big green lamp post
Said 'No more workin' brothers!
We'll leave them humings in the dark
And they'll bump into each other.

Just think about them walkin' round
With black eyes and broke noses
No more dogs to wet your feet
No more rusty toeses!

See, I've been a lamp post all me life, but
Now me mantles growin' dim,
They'll chuck me on the scrap heap
It's a shame! a crime! a sin! . . .

The other lamp posts muttered
And began to hiss and boo,
'Let's march upon the Town Hall
That's what we ought to do!'

The Lord Mayor he was woken
By a terribobble sight,
When he opened up his window
Didn't he get a fright!

There were twenty million lamp posts
And the light as bright as day
And the young lamp posts were shoutin' out
'Free Speech and Equal Pay! –

New Mantles Every Quarter!'
'I agree' the Lord Mayor cried
'To everything you ask for!'
Then he quickly ran inside.

So I watched the lamp posts go back home,
As quickly as they came
And with the first light of the day,
They were in their holes again.

Now there's an old age home for lamp posts
And an old age pension scheme
And every month they're painted
With a coat of glossy green,

New mantles every couple of months,
And they stand up straighter too,
And only the Lord Mayor knows why,
Him, and me, and twenty million lamp posts,

And a couple hundred dogs – and you.

Mike Harding

TREADIN' STEADY

Thrifty an' careful
John William Kaye
Browt up his youngsters
In t' similar way:
When he took 'em out walkin',
He'd cry, 'All together!
Lengthen your strides, lads,
An' save your boot-leather!'

William Beaumont

MI TWO AUNTS

Aunt Emma let us run around,
Aunt Lizzie made us sit;
Aunt Emma used to laugh a lot,
Aunt Lizzie, not a bit.

Aunt Lizzie had a lot to say,
But she talked ovver-mich
O' recent deaths an' buryins'
O' illnesses an' sich.

Aunt Emma made her currant-buns
So sweet an' fat an' nice,
Wi' currants plump an' plentiful
In ivvery tasty slice.

Aunt Lizzie's currant-buns were sad,
They nivver seemed to suit;
We fun' 'em short o' sweetenin',
An' allus short o' fruit.

Aunt Emma spread her butter thick,
Aunt Lizzie spread it thin;
– 'T were mostly to Aunt Emma's house
That we went visitin'!

William Beaumont

FIRST HAIKU OF SPRING

cuck oo cuck oo cuck
oo cuck oo cuck oo cuck oo
cuck oo cuck oo cuck

Roger McGough

WINDS LIGHT TO DISASTROUS

As I sipped morning tea,
A gale (force three)
Blew away a slice of toast.
Then a gale (force four)
Blew my wife out the door,
I wonder which I'll miss the most.
She was still alive
When a gale (force five)
Blew her screaming o'er Golders Green,
When a gale six blew
And it took her to
A mosque in the Medanine.
Now I pray to heaven
That a gale (force seven)
Will whisk her farther still,*
Let a gale (force eight)
Land her on the plate
Of a cannibal in Brazil.
As I sat down to dine
A gale (force Nine)
Blew away my chips & Spam
But! a gale (force ten)
Blew them back again,
What a lucky man I am!

Spike Milligan

*Father Still, a stationary priest

173

WINDY

The gale upon our holidays
Was not your passing breeze.
It gave our tents a fearful wrench
And bent the frantic trees.
So, if you've seen a flying tent,
And then observe another,
Please call us at your earliest,
We're also missing mother.

Max Fatchen

BALLOON

a s
big as
ball as round
as sun . . . I tug
and pull you when
you run and when
wind blows I
say polite
ly
H
O
L
D
M
E
T
I
G
H
T
L
Y.

Colleen Thibaudeau

PHEW! WHAT A SCORCHER!

It's seventy degrees:
In the shade
The cat waits to pounce
On dizzy sparrows;
In the sun
The house is undoing its buttons.

It's eighty degrees:
In the shade
The cat pretends to sleep
With one eye open;
In the sun
Tennis players are turning to ice cream.

It's nearly ninety;
In the sun
The grass gets sunburn
And begs the lawnmower to scratch its back;
In the shade
The cat
Sleeps.

David Orme

NOT A VERY CHEERFUL SONG, I'M AFRAID

There was a gloomy lady,
With a gloomy duck and a gloomy drake,
And they all three wandered gloomily,
Beside a gloomy lake,
On a gloomy, gloomy, gloomy, gloomy, gloomy, gloomy
day.

Now underneath that gloomy lake
The gloomy lady's gone.
But the gloomy duck and the gloomy drake
Swim on and on and on.
On a gloomy, gloomy, gloomy, gloomy, gloomy, gloomy
day.

Adrian Mitchell

IT'S NEVER FAIR WEATHER

I do not like the winter wind
That whistles from the North.
My upper teeth and those beneath
They jitter back and forth.
Oh, some are hanged, and some are skinned,
And others face the winter wind.

I do not like the summer sun
That scorches the horizon.
Though some delight in Fahrenheit,
To me it's deadly pizen.
I think that life would be more fun
Without the simmering summer sun.

I do not like the signs of spring,
The fever and the chills,
The icy mud, the puny bud,
The frozen daffodils.
Let other poets gaily sing;
I do not like the signs of spring.

I do not like the foggy fall
That strips the maples bare;
The radiator's mating call,
The dank, rheumatic air;
I fear that taken all in all,
I do not like the foggy fall.

The winter sun, of course, is kind,
And summer's wind a saviour,
And I'll merrily sing of fall and spring
When they're on their good behaviour.
But otherwise I see no reason
To speak in praise of any season.

Ogden Nash

DEATH OF A SNOWMAN

I was awake all night,
Big as a polar bear,
Strong and firm and white.
The tall black hat I wear
Was draped with ermine fur.
I felt so fit and well
Till the world began to stir
And the morning sun swell.
I was tired, began to yawn;
At noon in the humming sun
I caught a severe warm;
My nose began to run.
My hat grew black and fell,
Was followed by my grey head.
There was no funeral bell,
But by tea-time I was dead.

Vernon Scannell

WINTER MORNING

Winter is the king of showmen,
Turning tree stumps into snow men
And houses into birthday cakes
And spreading sugar over lakes.
Smooth and clean and frosty white,
The world looks good enough to bite.
That's the season to be young,
Catching snowflakes on your tongue.
Snow is snowy when it's snowing,
I'm sorry it's slushy when it's going.

Ogden Nash

THE SNOWMAN

Mother, while you were at the shops
and I was snoozing in my chair
I heard a tap at the window
saw a snowman standing there

He looked so cold and miserable
I almost could have cried
so I put the kettle on
and invited him inside

I made him a cup of cocoa
to warm the cockles of his nose
then he snuggled in front of the fire
for a cosy little doze

He lay there warm and smiling
softly counting sheep
I eavesdropped for a little while
then I too fell asleep

Seems he awoke and tiptoed out
exactly when I'm not too sure
it's a wonder you didn't see him
as you came in through the door

(oh, and by the way,
the kitten's made a puddle on the floor)

Roger McGough

IT'S SPRING, IT'S SPRING

It's spring, it's spring –

when everyone sits round a roaring fire
telling ghost stories!

It's spring, it's spring –

when everyone sneaks into everyone else's yard
and bashes up their snowman!

It's spring, it's spring –

when the last dead leaves fall from the trees
and Granny falls off your toboggan!

It's spring, it's spring –

when you'd give your right arm
for a steaming hot bowl of soup!

It's spring, it's spring –

when you'd give your right leg
not to be made to wash up after Christmas dinner!

It's spring, it's spring –

isn't it?

Kit Wright

WINDSHIELD WIPERS

Windshield wipers
Wipe away the rain,
Please bring the sunshine
Back again.

Windshield wipers
Clean our car,
The fields are green
And we're travelling far.

My father's coat is warm
My mother's lap is deep
Windshield wipers
Carry me to sleep.

And when I wake,
The sun will be
A golden home
Surrounding me;

But if that rain gets worse
Gets worse instead,
I want to sleep
Till I'm in bed.

Windshield wipers
Wipe away the rain,
Please bring the sunshine
Back again.

Dennis Lee

ECLIPSE

I looked the sun straight in the eye
He put on dark glasses

F. R. Scott

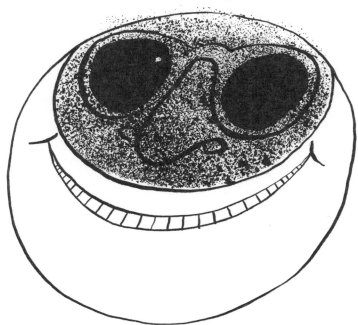

THE WIND AND THE MOON

Said the Wind to the Moon,
'I will blow you out;
    You stare
    In the air
    Like a ghost in a chair
Always looking what I am about.
I hate to be watched – I'll blow
            you out.'

George MacDonald

185

ALL THE TIME

If
we dug a hole
through the moon
we could have light
all the time.

The sun
would shine
through
at night.

Ivor Cutler

THE AIR

The air was once about to die.

It cried: 'O help me, Lord on high;
I am distressed and feeling sick,
am getting sluggish, getting thick;
you always know a way, Papa:
send me abroad, or to a spa,
or buttermilk may cure and heal –
else to the devil I'll appeal!'

The Lord, perturbed by this affair,
invented 'sound massage for air.'

Since then the world is full of noise,
which thrivingly the air enjoys.

Christian Morgenstern

THE TWO ROOTS

A pair of pine roots, old and dark,
make conversation in the park.

The whispers where the top leaves grow
are echoed in the roots below.

An agèd squirrel sitting there
is knitting stockings for the pair.

The one says: squeak. The other: squawk.
That is enough for one day's talk.

Christian Morgenstern

THE HOUSE ON THE HILL

It was built years ago
by someone quite manic
and sends those who go there
away in blind panic.
They tell tales of horrors
that can injure or kill
designed by the madman
who lived on the hill.

> If you visit the House on the Hill for a dare
> remember my words . . .
> > 'There are dangers. Beware!'

The piano's white teeth
when you plonk out a note
will bite off your fingers
then reach for your throat.
The living room curtains
– long, heavy and black –
will wrap you in cobwebs
if you're slow to step back.

> If you enter the House on the Hill for a dare
> remember my words . . .
> > 'There are dangers. Beware!'

The 'fridge in the kitchen
has a self-closing door.
If it knocks you inside
then you're ice cubes . . . for sure.
The steps to the cellar
are littered with bones,
and up from the darkness
drift creakings and groans.

IS ANYB-B-BODY THERE?

189

If you go to the House on the Hill for a dare
remember my words . . .

                   'There are dangers. Beware!'

Turn on the hot tap
and the bathroom will flood
not with gallons of water
but litres of blood.
The rocking-chair's arms
can squeeze you to death;
a waste of time shouting
as you run . . . out . . . of . . . breath.

Don't say you weren't warned or told to take care
when you entered the House on the Hill . . .

                                   for a dare.

                              Wes Magee

BUMP

Things that go 'bump' in the night
Should not really give one a fright.
It's the hole in each ear
That lets in the fear,
That, and the absence of light!

Spike Milligan

HANDSAW

HANDSAWWWWWWWWWWWWWWWW

Richard Lebovitz

VLAD

Vlad ve
vampire vlies
vrough voonlight
velvet vat vings vlitter-
vlutter. Vlad's very vain vith
vangs vo vlong vey vite
vrough vlesh vlike vutter.
Vlad vears a vast vile
violet vest villed vith
vermin vrom va vault
vich vongs vorse·van
virty vultures – vo
vonder victims
vaint   vand
vall! Vicious,
vulgar, vlood-
vrinking, vad,
v i o l e n t ,
villainous-
vot a vlad

Dave Calder

THE MOON

The moon paints faces on the houses,
Gives them eyes and gives them mouthses
Paints a grin where there was none
And now that things of day are gone

He stretches shadows on the midden,
And jumps the cats from where they're hidden
He silvers puddles, gilds the cobbles
And makes my shadow twitch and hobble

And limp behind me through the park
The moon makes daydreams of the dark
And when you're walking past old statues
He makes them wink and then come at you.

If ever on moonlit nights I roam
I always wish that I'd stayed home.

Mike Harding

COLONEL FAZACKERLEY

Colonel Fazackerley Butterworth-Toast
Bought an old castle complete with a ghost,
But someone or other forgot to declare
To Colonel Fazack that the spectre was there.

On the very first evening, while waiting to dine,
The Colonel was taking a fine sherry wine,
When the ghost, with a furious flash and a flare,
Shot out of the chimney and shivered, 'Beware!'

Colonel Fazackerley put down his glass
And said, 'My dear fellow, that's really first class!
I just can't conceive how you do it at all.
I imagine you're going to a Fancy Dress Ball?'

At this, the dread ghost gave a withering cry.
Said the Colonel (his monocle firm in his eye),
'Now just how you do it I wish I could think.
Do sit down and tell me, and please have a drink.'

The ghost in his phosphorous cloak gave a roar
And floated about between ceiling and floor.
He walked through a wall and returned through a pane
And backed up the chimney and came down again.

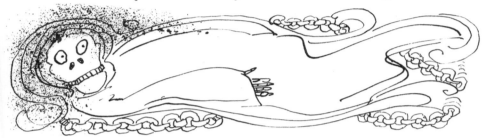

Said the Colonel, 'With laughter I'm feeling quite weak!'
(As trickles of merriment ran down his cheek).
'My house-warming party I hope you won't spurn.
You *must* say you'll come and you'll give us a turn!'

At this, the poor spectre – quite out of his wits –
Proceeded to shake himself almost to bits.
He rattled his chains and he clattered his bones
And he filled the whole castle with mumbles and moans.

But Colonel Fazackerley, just as before,
Was simply delighted and called out, 'Encore!'
At which the ghost vanished, his efforts in vain,
And never was seen at the castle again.

'Oh dear, what a pity!' said Colonel Fazack.
'I don't know his name, so I can't call him back.'
And then with a smile that was hard to define,
Colonel Fazackerley went in to dine.

Charles Causley

THE STRANGE WILD SONG

He thought he saw a Buffalo,
    Upon the chimney-piece:
He looked again, and found it was
    His Sister's Husband's Niece.
'Unless you leave this house,' he said,
    'I'll send for the Police!'

He thought he saw a Rattlesnake,
    That questioned him in Greek;
He looked again, and found it was
    The Middle of Next Week.
'The one thing I regret,' he said,
    'Is that it cannot speak!'

He thought he saw a Banker's Clerk
   Descending from a bus;
He looked again, and found it was
   A Hippopotamus.
'If this should stay to dine,' he said,
   'There won't be much for us!'

He thought he saw a Kangaroo
   That worked a coffee mill:
He looked again, and found it was
   A Vegetable Pill.
'Were I to swallow this,' he said,
   'I should be very ill!'

He thought he saw a Coach-and-four
   That stood beside his bed;
He looked again, and found it was
   A Bear without a Head;
'Poor thing,' he said, 'poor silly thing!
   It's waiting to be fed!'

He thought he saw an Albatross
   That fluttered round the Lamp;
He looked again, and found it was
   A Penny-Postage-Stamp.
'You'd best be getting home,' he said,
   'The nights are very damp!'

Lewis Carroll

WHO'S THAT

Who's that
stopping at
my door in the
dark, deep in the dead of the moonless night?

Who's
that in the quiet
blackness, darker than dark?

Who
turns the han-
dle of my door, who
turns the old brass hand-
le of
my door with never a sound, the handle
that always creaks and rattles and
squeaks but
now
turns
without a sound, slowly
slowly,
   slowly
     round?

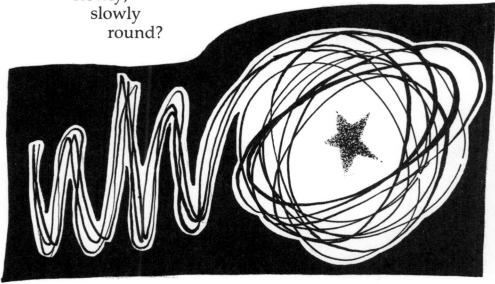

Who's that moving through the floor
as if it were a lake, an open door? Who
is it who passes through
what can never be passed through?
who passes through
the rocking-chair
without rocking it,
who passes through
the table without knocking it, who
walks out of the cupboard without unlocking it?
Who's that? Who plays with my toys
with no noise, no
noise?

Who's that? Who is it
silent and silver
as things in mirrors, who's
as slow as feathers,
shy as the shivers,
light as a fly?

Who's that who's that
as close as
close as a hug, a kiss –

Who's THIS?

James Kirkup

WELL, IT'S TODAY ALREADY

Well, it's today already.

I don't know how it got here,
but there's a funny echo in this room.   room

Martin Hall

TROLL

I'm a troll, foldy roll,
and I'm standing on my bridge.
I'm a troll, foldy roll,
and there's nothing in my fridge.
And I'm getting very hungry
For a nice sam-widge.
So I'll slap you on a slice
and I'll bite – SQUELCH! SQUIDGE!

Or I'll roll you and I'll fold you
in a big foldy roll.
Then I'll lick you and I'll stick you
in my great cake-hole.

I'm a troll, foldy roll,
and I aren't half strong.
And I'm big and I'm hairy
and I don't half pong.
And I gobble up people
though it's nasty and it's wrong.
Now it's time to give a roll
on my noisy dinner GONG!

Tony Mitton

BEWARE

This cunning creature in its lair,
You'll find, is lurking everywhere.
There may be one (or even two).
It could be sitting next to you.
With staring eyes it's on the prowl.
It gives a sudden roar (or howl)
And, in a flash, to your dismay
It's leaping forward to its prey.
Beware each night this fearful danger –
The dreaded telly channel changer.

Max Fatchen

THE LOCH NESS MONSTER'S SONG

Sssnnnwhufffll?
Hnwhuffl hhnnwfl hnfl hfl?
Gdroblboblhobngbl gbl gl g g g g glbgl.
Drublhaflablhaflubhafgabhaflhafl fl fl –
gm grawwwww grf grawf awfgm graw gm.
Hovoplodok-doplodovok-plovodokot-doplodokosh?
Splgraw fok fok splgrafhatchgabrlgabrl fok splfok!
Zgra kra gka fok!
Grof grawff gahf?
Gombl mbl bl –
blm plm,
blm plm,
blm plm,
blp.

Edwin Morgan

O HERE IT IS! AND THERE IT IS!

O here it is! And there it is!
And no one knows whose share it is
Nor dares to stake a claim –
But we have seen it in the air
A fairy like a William Pear –
With but itself to blame.

A thug it is – and smug it is
And like a floating pug it is
Above the orchard trees
It has no right – no right at all
To soar above the orchard wall
With chilblains on its knees.

Mervyn Peake

SOME ONE

Some one came knocking
    At my wee, small door;
Some one came knocking,
    I'm sure – sure – sure;

I listened, I opened,
    I looked to left and right,
But nought there was a-stirring
    In the still dark night;

Only the busy beetle
    Tap-tapping in the wall,
Only from the forest
    The screech-owl's call,

Only the cricket whistling
    While the dewdrops fall,
So I know not who came knocking,
    At all, at all, at all.

Walter de la Mare

DON'T BE SCARED

The dark is only a blanket
for the moon to put on her bed.

The dark is a private cinema
for the movie dreams in your head.

The dark is a little black dress
to show off the sequin stars.

The dark is the wooden hole
behind the strings of happy guitars.

The dark is a jeweller's velvet cloth
where children sleep like pearls.

The dark is a spool of film
to photograph boys and girls,

so smile in your sleep in the dark.
Don't be scared.

Carol Ann Duffy

SO BIG!

The dinosaur, an ancient beast,
I'm told, was very large.
His eyes were big as billiard balls,
His stomach, a garage.
He had a huge and humping back,
A neck as long as Friday.
I'm glad he lived so long ago
And doesn't live in my day!

Max Fatchen

THE DINOSAURS ARE NOT ALL DEAD

The dinosaurs are not all dead.
I saw one raise its iron head
To watch me walking down the road
Beyond our house today.
Its jaws were dripping with a load
Of earth and grass that it had cropped.
It must have heard me where I stopped,
Snorted white steam my way,
And stretched its long neck out to see,
And chewed, and grinned quite amiably.

Charles Malam

ELEPHANT

It is quite unfair to be
obliged to be so large, so I suppose
you could call me discontented.

Think big, they said, when
I was a little elephant; they
wanted to get me used to it.

It was kind. But it doesn't help if,
inside, you are carefree in small ways,
fond of little amusements.

You are smaller than me, think
how conveniently near the flowers are,
how you can pat the cat by just

halfbending over. You can also
arrange teacups for dolls, play
marbles in the proper season.

I would give anything to be
able to do a tiny, airy, flitting
dance to show how very little a

thing happiness can be really.

Alan Brownjohn

WHEN THERE'S A FIRE IN THE JUNGLE

When there's a fire in the jungle,
They call the Elephant Brigade,
Who race with their trunks full of water,
To the place that has to be sprayed.
But if the fire is a big one,
It happens as often as not,
That the elephants drink all the water,
To stop themselves getting too hot.

Martin Honeysett

ELEPHANTS

Elephants

aren't any more important
than insects

but I'm on the side
of elephants

unless one of them tries
to crawl up my leg

John Newlove

THE HAIRY-NOSED PREPOSTEROUS

The Hairy-Nosed Preposterous
Looks much like a Rhinosterous,
But also something like a tank—
For which he has himself to thank.

His ears are the size of tennis shoes,
His eyes the size of pins.
And when he lies down for a snooze
An orchestra begins.

It whistles, rattles, roars, and thumps,
And the wind of it comes and goes
Through the storm-tossed hair that grows in clumps
On the end of his capable nose.

John Ciardi

THE HIPPOPOTAMUS

Consider the poor hippopotamus:
His life is unduly monotonous.
He lives half asleep
At the edge of the deep,
And his face is as big as his bottom is.

Anonymous

A SEA-SERPENT SAW A BIG TANKER

A sea-serpent saw a big tanker,
Bit a hole in her side and then sank her.
    It swallowed the crew
    In a minute or two,
And then picked its teeth with the anchor.

Anonymous

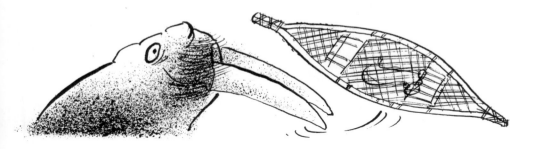

THE WALRUS

The Walrus lives on icy floes
And unsuspecting Eskimoes.

Don't bring your wife to Arctic Tundra
A Walrus may bob up from undra.

Michael Flanders

THE TRUTH ABOUT THE ABOMINABLE FOOTPRINT

The Yeti's a Beast
Who lives in the East
   And suffers a lot from B.O.
His hot hairy feet
Stink out the street
   So he cools them off in the snow.

Michael Baldwin

TIBETAN LAMENT

The loveliest of our lamas
Is gone beyond the door.
He'll never wear pyjamas
Any more, any more.

Above the yawning chasm
He tried to pass a yak;
It took a sneezing spasm
And blew him off his track.
Now the silent valley has him,
And he can't come back.

The loveliest of our lamas
Is gone beyond the door.
He'll never wear pyjamas
Any more.

Anonymous

THE CHEETAH, MY DEAREST, IS KNOWN NOT TO CHEAT

The cheetah, my dearest, is known not to cheat;
the tiger possesses no tie;
the horse-fly, of course, was never a horse;
the lion will not tell a lie.

The turkey, though perky, was never a Turk;
nor the monkey ever a monk;
the mandrel, though like one, was never a man,
but some men are like him, when drunk.

The springbok, dear thing, was not born in the Spring;
the walrus will not build a wall.
No badger is bad; no adder can add.
There is no truth in these things at all.

George Barker

COWS

The cows that browse in pastures
Seem not at all surprised
That as they moo they mow the lawn
And their milk comes pasture-ized.

X. J. Kennedy

A COW'S OUTSIDE

A cow's outside is mainly hide,
undoubtedly this leather
retains a cow's insides inside,
and holds a cow together.

Jack Prelutsky

LONELY IN A FIELD

The hen it is a noble beast
But a cow is more forlorner
Standing lonely in a field
Wi' one leg at each corner.

MacAnon.

217

THE LESSON

Of all the fleas that ever flew
(And flying fleas are rather few
((Because for proper flying you
(((Whether you are a flea or not)))
Need wings and things fleas have not got)))—

(I make the further point that fleas
Are thick as these parentheses
((An illustration (((you'll agree)))
Both apt and pleasing to a flea)))—

Now then where were we? Let me see—
Ah, yes.—We said to fly you ought
(Whether you are a flea or not)
To have some wings (yes, at least two
((At least no less than two will do
(((And fleas have something less than one
((((One less, in fact (((((or frankly, none))))
(((((Which, as once more you will agree)))))
Limits the flying of a flea))))))))).

And let me add that fleas that fly
Are known as Flears. (You can see why.)

All I have said thus far is true.
(If it's not clear, that's up to you.
((You'll have to learn sometime, my dear,
That what is true may not be clear
(((While what is clear may not be true
((((And you'll be wiser when you do.)))))))))

John Ciardi

EARWIG

The horny goloch is an awesome beast
supple and scaly:
It has two horns, and a hantle of feet
And a forkie tailie.

MacAnon.

THE SCORPION

The scorpion is as black as soot,
  He dearly loves to bite;
He is a most unpleasant brute
  To find in bed, at night.

Hilaire Belloc

LOVELY MOSQUITO

Lovely mosquito, attacking my arm
As quiet and still as a statue,
Stay right where you are! I'll do you no harm –
I simply desire to pat you.

Just puncture my veins and swallow your fill
For nobody's going to swot you.
Now, lovely mosquito, stay perfectly still –
A SWIPE! and a SPLAT! and I GOT YOU!

Doug Macleod

WHEN ROVER PASSED OVER

When Rover died, my sister cried;
I tried my best to calm her.
I said, 'We'll have him mummified,
I know a good embalmer.'

And so we packed the wretched pup
Into a wicker basket.
We duly had him bandaged up,
And kept him in a casket.

Now Rover we will not forget,
Though he is but a dummy.
For though we've lost a faithful pet,
We've gained an extra Mummy!

Colin West

PUSSYCAT, PUSSYCAT

Pussycat, pussycat, where have you been,
Licking your lips with your whiskers so clean?
Pussycat, pussycat, purring and pudgy,
Pussycat, pussycat. WHERE IS OUR BUDGIE?

Max Fatchen

CONVERSATION ON A GARDEN WALL

Move over, you've got all the bricks with the sun on.

Oh, all right. Mind you, I was here first.

He came round after me again last night. Right up to the back door.

Really? He's persistent, I'll say that for him.

I'll say. Anyway, they chased him away.

How are yours treating you?

Not too bad, really. They're a bit careful with the milk.

Oh, mine are all right about that. They're a bit unimaginative with my food, though. Last week I had the same meal every day.

You don't say. The food's O.K. It's a real pain being pushed out in the rain. Every night, rain or snow, out I go.

Me too. Look, here he is back again.

Cheek. Pretend to take no notice.

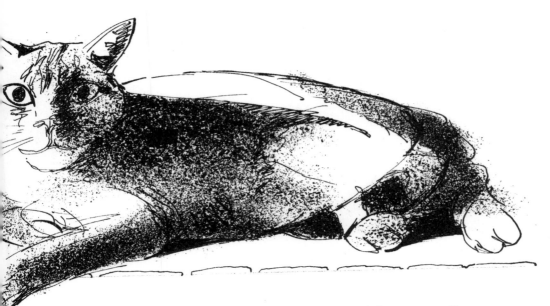

At least you've got a quiet place with none of those small ones around. I hardly get a minute.

That's true. All mine do is sit in front of a little box with tiny ones inside it.

Mine do too. It's the only peace I get.

And one of them pushes that noisy thing round the floor every day.

Terrible, isn't it? Mind you, mine only does it once or twice a week.

You're lucky. Oh, the sun's gone in.

Yes, time for a stroll. I'll jump down and just sort of walk past him, accidentally.

Accidentally on purpose, you mean. See you around.

Yes, see you around. I'll tell you one thing, though.

What's that?

It's a good job they can't talk, isn't it?

Adrian Henri

SOMEONE STOLE THE

While I was taking a short   -nap
    someone stole the   ,
I should have spun round like a   herine wheel
    when someone stole the   .
But I was too slow to   ch them,
    when someone stole the   .

Now the   amaran can't float,
    because someone stole the   .
And the   erpillar can't crawl,
    because someone stole the   .
And the   aract can't fall,
    because someone stole the   .

It was not me and it was not you
    but it is   egorically true,
And if you were to ask me
    I'd say it was a   astrophe
That someone's stolen the   .

Brian Patten

BAT CHANT

I'm a bat
furry bat
and I'm happy as Larry in the dark
'Cos I got radar, I don't need eyesight
I dip and I loop
In the dovegray twilight
I zip and I swoop
in the navyblue midnight
but I'm over the moon when its black as pitch.
Come the dawn I'll be gone
but at sunset I start to twitch
when my folded up wings begin to itch
for the dark,
pitch dark.
No I'm not a
spooky moth, no I'm not a
sort of
night bird not a flying mouse
though I fly and I squeak in my hollowtree house
I'm a bat
fancy that,
highnoon
I hang upside down like a sunny day umbrella
waiting for dark
wait till night is as
dark as the big black cloak of Dracula
I'm a bat
I'm unique
from my highpitch unaided hearing and my supersonic
                                                    squeak
I'm a bat
and I'm happy as Larry in the dark.

Liz Lochhead

225

BATTY

The baby bat
Screamed out in fright,
'Turn on the dark,
I'm afraid of the light.'

Shel Silverstein

THE HAWK

Afternoon,
with just enough of a breeze
            for him to ride it
lazily, a hawk
sails still-winged
up the slope of a stubble-covered hill,
so low
he nearly
touches his shadow

Robert Sund

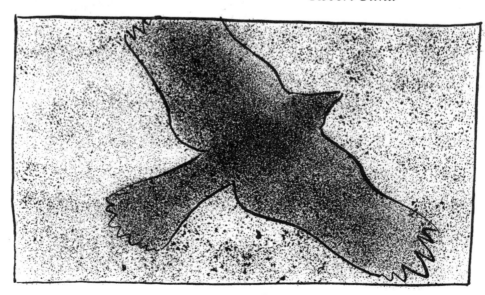

THE TICKLE RHYME

'Who's that tickling my back?'
        said the wall.
'Me,' said a small
Caterpillar. 'I'm learning
To crawl.'

Ian Serraillier

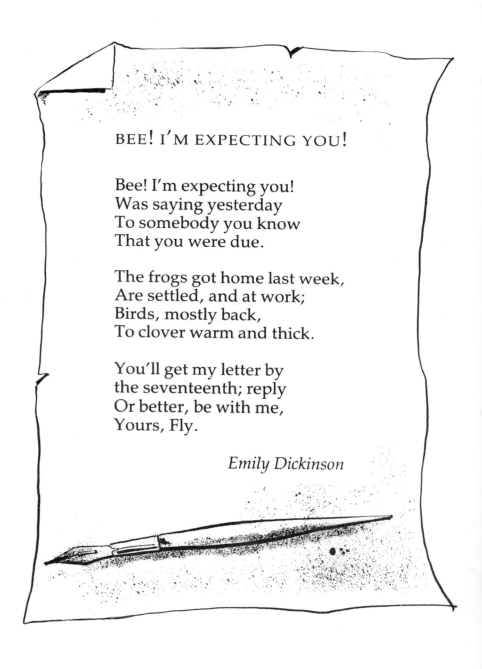

BEE! I'M EXPECTING YOU!

Bee! I'm expecting you!
Was saying yesterday
To somebody you know
That you were due.

The frogs got home last week,
Are settled, and at work;
Birds, mostly back,
To clover warm and thick.

You'll get my letter by
the seventeenth; reply
Or better, be with me,
Yours, Fly.

Emily Dickinson

ANT AND ELEPH-ANT

Said a tiny Ant
To the Elephant,
'Mind how you tread in this clearing!'

But alas! Cruel fate!
She was crushed by the weight
Of an Elephant, hard of hearing.

Spike Milligan

ANTEATER

Anteater, Anteater
Where have you been?
Aunt Liz took you walkies
And hasn't been seen.

Nor has Aunt Mary,
Aunt Flo or Aunt Di.
Anteater, Anteater
Why the gleam in your eye?

S. K. Werp

FRENCH VERSION

Tantemanger, Tantemanger
Comment allez-vous?
Tante Claire se promenait,
Et a disparu.

Aussi Tante Marie,
Tantes Simone et Lulu.
Tantemanger, Tantemanger,
Pourquoi souriez-vous?

Roger McGough

A CRUEL MAN A BEETLE CAUGHT

A cruel man a beetle caught,
And to the wall him pinned, oh!
Then said the beetle to the crowd,
'Though I'm stuck up I am not proud,'
And his soul went out of the window.

Anonymous

HOUSE FLIES

What makes
common house flies
trying
is
that they keep
multiflieing

Niels Mogens Bodecker

THE FLY

God in his wisdom made the fly
And then forgot to tell us why.

Ogden Nash

GIGL

a pigl
wigl
if
u
tigl

Arnold Spilka

THE TERNS

Said the mother Tern
    to her baby Tern
Would you like a brother?
Said baby Tern
    to mother Tern
Yes
One good Tern deserves another.

Spike Milligan

THE TORTOISE AND THE HARE

Languid, lethargic, listless and slow,
The tortoise would dally, an image of sloth.
'Immobile', 'Stagnant', to the hare it was both.

'Enough of your insults, I seek satisfaction.
I'll run you a race and win by a fraction.'
Thus challenged the tortoise one afternoon.
'Right,' said the hare, 'and let it be soon.'

They decided they'd race right through the wood,
And the tortoise set off as fast as it could.
The hare followed at a leisurely pace
Quite confident that it could win the race.

The tortoise thought as it ambled along,
'I have never been faster, or quite so strong.'
The hare on the other hand was often inclined
To stop at the wayside and improve its mind.

It read a fable by Aesop deep in the wood,
Then of course it set off as fast as it could.
It decided it would put that fable aright
As it sped along with the speed of light.

Languid, lethargic, listless and slow
The tortoise ran fast as a tortoise could go.
Yet the hare having decided on saving face
Quite easily managed to win the race.

'I feel,' said the tortoise, 'that I have been deceived,
For fables are things I have always believed.
I would love to have won a race clearly designed
To point out a moral both old and refined.'

'Losing a race would not matter,' the hare said,
'For in speed Mother Nature placed me ahead.
Some fables are things you ought to contest,
Dear Tortoise, in mine, I'm afraid you've come last.'

Brian Patten

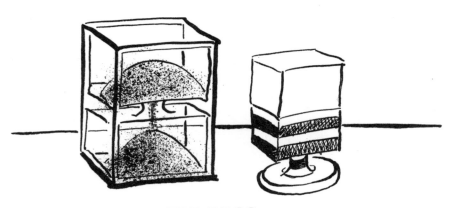

SKWERP EGGS
(in round holes)

Have you ever seen
a skwerp?

Ever heard its plain-
tive cry? (skwerp! skwerp!)

Ever tasted a
skwerp egg?

Delicious. Give one
a try.

Fry gently in a
square pan

(why not a round one?
won't fit)

cut neatly into
four cubes

say grace, then eat
every bit (slurp! slurp!)

S. K. Werp

235

A NURSE MOTIVATED BY SPITE

A nurse motivated by spite
Tied her infantine charge to a kite;
 She launched it with ease
 On the afternoon breeze,
And watched till it flew out of sight.

Edward Gorey

A CERTAIN YOUNG MAN IT WAS NOTED

A certain young man, it was noted,
Went about in the heat thickly-coated;
    He said, 'You may scoff,
    But I shan't take it off;
Underneath I am horribly bloated.'

Edward Gorey

BRENDA BAKER

Brenda Baker, quite ill-bred,
Used to cuddle fish in bed.
Tuna, trout and conger-eels,
Salmon, sole and sometimes seals.
Barracuda, bream and bass,
She cuddled them, until – alas!
One unforgotten Friday night
She slept with two piranhas,
And, being rather impolite,
They ate her best pyjamas!

Doug Macleod

ANNA ELISE

Anna Elise, she jumped with surprise;
The surprise was so quick, it played her a trick;
The trick was so rare, she jumped in a chair;
The chair was so frail she jumped in a pail;
The pail was so wet, she jumped in a net;
The net was so small, she jumped on the ball;
The ball was so round, she jumped on the ground;
And ever since then she's been turning around.

Anonymous

MR KARTOFFEL

Mr Kartoffel's a whimsical man;
He drinks his beer from a watering-can,
And for no good reason that I can see
He fills his pockets with china tea.
He parts his hair with a knife and fork
And takes his ducks for a Sunday walk.
Says he, 'If my wife and I should choose
To wear our stockings outside our shoes,
Plant tulip bulbs in the baby's pram
And eat tobacco instead of jam,
And fill the bath with cauliflowers,
That's nobody's business at all but ours.'

James Reeves

OLD HANK

For a lark,
For a prank,
Old Hank
Walked a plank.
These bubbles mark
O
O
O
O
O
Where Hank sank.

Anonymous

GENERAL GERALD

When General Gerald gets dressed,
A hundred medals are pinned to his chest.

One is for valor.
One is for zeal.
One is for swallowing all his oatmeal.

One's from Sumatra.
One's from Tangiers.
One is for cleaning behind his ears.

One is for trust.
One is for honor.
One is for looking just like an iguana.

One is for spirit.
One is for poise.
One is for sharing his games and his toys.

Douglas Florian

FAME

The best thing
about being famous

is when you walk
down the street

and people turn round
to look at you

and bump into things.

Roger McGough

INDEX OF POETS

INDEX OF FIRST LINES

247

248

252

ACKNOWLEDGMENTS

The publisher would like to thank the copyright holders for permission to reproduce the following copyright material:

Allan Ahlberg: Penguin Books Ltd for "I Did a Bad Thing Once", "Picking Teams" and "Supply Teacher" from *Please Mrs Butler* by Allan Ahlberg, Kestrel, 1983. Copyright © Allan Ahlberg. **Michael Baldwin**: the author for "The Truth about the Abominable Footprint". Copyright © Michael Baldwin. **George Barker**: Faber and Faber Ltd for "The Cheetah, My Dearest" from *Runes and Rhymes and Tunes and Chimes* by George Barker. **Hilaire Belloc**: "Matilda", "The Python", and "The Scorpion" from *Cautionary Tales* by Hilaire Belloc. Reprinted by permission of PFD on behalf of The Estate of Hilaire Belloc. Copyright © Hilaire Belloc. **Carey Blyton**: the author for "Night Starvation" by Carey Blyton from *Bananas in Pyjamas*. Copyright © Carey Blyton. **Niels Mogens Bodecker**: "House Flies" reprinted with the permission of Margaret K. McElderry Books, an imprint of Simon & Schuster Children's Publishing Division from *Hurry, Hurry, Mary Dear! And Other Nonsense Poems* by N. M. Bodecker. Copyright © 1976 N. M. Bodecker. **Keith Bosley**: the author for "The Fastest Train in the World" by Keith Bosley, from *And I Dance*. Copyright © Keith Bosley. **Alan Brownjohn**: Macmillan Publishers Ltd for "Elephant" from *Brownjohn's Beasts* by Alan Brownjohn. **Charles Causley**: David Higham Associates for "Colonel Fazackerley" from *Figgie Hobbin: Poems for Nine Year Olds and Under* by Charles Causley, Macmillan. **William Cole**: The Estate of William Cole for "The Cruel Naughty Boy" and "Lost Contact". **John Collis**: the author for "Job Satisfaction". Copyright © John Collis. **Billy Connolly**: the author for "I'd Rather Be a Sausage" by Billy Connolly. **Wendy Cope**: Faber and Faber Ltd for "Kenneth" from *Uncollected Poems* by Wendy Cope. **Ivor Cutler**: the author for "All the Time", "Killer Bees", and "Piranhas" by Ivor Cutler. **Jan Dean**: the author for "The Rubber Plant Speaks" by Jan Dean. **Walter de la Mare**: The Literary Trustees of Walter de la Mare and the Society of Authors as their representative for "Some One" by Walter de la Mare from *The Complete Poems of Walter de la Mare*. **Peter Dixon**: the author for "Colour of My Dreams" from *Colour of My Dreams*, Pan Macmillan, 2002; "I'd Like to Be a Teabag" and "Questions" from *Grow Your Own Poems*, Pedre Luna, 1999. Copyright © Peter Dixon. **Denis Doyle**: Susan Doyle on behalf of Denis Doyle for "Shirley Said" from *Apricot Rhymes* by Denis Doyle. Copyright © Denis Doyle. **Gavin Ewart**: the author for "Xmas for the Boys" from *The Collected Ewart 1933–1980* by Gavin Ewart, Hutchinson. Copyright © Gavin Ewart. **Max Fatchen**: John Johnson (Authors' Agent) Limited for "Jump Over the Moon" (Nutty Nursery Rhymes), "Look Out!" and "So Big" from *Songs for My Dog and Other People* by Max Fatchen, Kestrel 1980; "Beware", "Ears", "Pussycat, Pussycat" and "Windy" from *Wry Rhymes for Troublesome Times* by Max Fatchen, Kestrel 1983. Copyright © Max Fatchen. **Roy Fuller**: John Fuller for "Advice to Children" by Roy Fuller. Copyright © John Fuller. **Edward Gorey**: The Estate of Edward Gorey for "A Certain Young Man It Was Noted", "A Nurse Motivated by Spite", and "A Lady Born under a Curse" from *The Listing Attic* by Edward Gorey. Copyright © 1954 by Edward Gorey. **Mick Gowar**: Collins Publishers for "Christmas Thank You's" from *Swings and Roundabouts* by Mick Gowar. **Harry Graham**: "Quiet Fun" by Harry Graham, from *Ruthless Rhymes for Heartless Homes*, Edward Arnold. **Robert Graves**: Carcanet Press Limited for "The Hero" from *Complete Poems* by Robert Graves. **Mike Harding**: "Advice to Grownups and Other Animals", "The Moon", "The Revolt of the Lamp Posts" and "My Uncle Fudge Told Lies" by Mike Harding, from *Up the Boo Aye, Shooting Pookakies*. Copyright © Mike Harding. **Gregory Harrison**: the author for "Distracted the Mother Said to Her Boy". **John Hegley**: PFD on behalf of John Hegley for "Contact Lenses" and "Uncle and Auntie" from *Visions of the Bone Idol*. Copyright © John Hegley. **Adrian Henri**: the author c/o Rogers, Coleridge & White Ltd., 20 Powis Mews, London W11 1JN for "Conversation on a Garden Wall" and "Marigolds" by Adrian Henri, from *The Phantom Lollipop Lady*, Methuen 1986. Copyright © Adrian Henri 1986. **Russell Hoban**: the author and the publisher for "The Friendly Cinnamon Bun" from *The Pedalling Man* by Russell Hoban, Heinemann. **Sidney Hoddes**: the author for "Mashed Potato / Love Poem". Copyright © Sidney Hoddes. **Martin Honeysett**: "When There's a Fire in the Jungle" from *What a Lot of Nonsense!* edited by John Foster. First published by Methuen Children's Books and used with permission of Egmont Children's Books Limited, London. **Ted Hughes**: Faber and Faber Ltd for "Grandma" from *Meet My Folks* by Ted Hughes. **X. J. Kennedy**: "Cows" Copyright © 1975 by X. J. Kennedy. Excerpt from *One Winter Night in August and Other Nonsense Jingles*, published by Margaret K. McElderry Books. Reprinted by permission of Curtis Brown, Ltd. **James Kirkup**: the author for "Who's That". **Dennis Lee**: "Windshield Wipers" from *Alligator Pie* by Dennis Lee. Reprinted by permission of Macmillan of Canada, A Division of Canada